True honor is an outflow from a heart that fe
friend Gary walk out the truths contained in th
es, Gary expounds on the kingdom principle o
lock the gifts in others, but will also release G

-Jonn Bevere
Best-selling Author and Minister
Co-founder of Messenger International

Honor! Don't get tired of that word because that is the core message of my friend Gary Montoya's book Kingdom Honor. Gary is absolutely on target when he says, "Honor will give you direct access to God." I have no doubt that the Kingdom of our Lord will be strengthened as volunteers and leaders understand the ultimate role of honor in the Church. You and all your Christian leader friends will want this book.

-**Sam Chand**
Leadership Consultant and author of Leadership Pain

Honor is such a vital kingdom value for life as God intended us to live it. With conviction, this book comprehensively covers how honor shapes the church to become all that it was designed to be. Gary explores and expounds it in a way that leaves no room for misunderstanding, misappropriation or excuse. This resource is a blessing to everyone who follows Christ and I highly recommend it.

-**Mark Varughese**
Founder & Senior Leader of Kingdomcity

I believe that one of the keys that is keeping so many believers from ever entering into the fullness of their calling is not understanding honor. I've witnessed many over my decades of ministry hit that ceiling and it's simply a result of their inability to honor their previous pastor, leader, or authority in their life. I believe that God is raising up a new breed of people in this hour who are going to move in a different spirit and connect to the glory and power of honor. I highly recommend this book by my friend Gary Montoya!

-**Corey Russell**
Author of "Teach us to Pray"

I am so honored to endorse "Kingdom Honor", written by my friend pastor/author Gary Montoya. He has truly exemplified and lived a life of honor and servanthood. I believe this book is a must read for all that desire to be used greatly by God. I have always said that "submission is just a theory until it costs you something." Gary reminds us that to be truly great in God's Kingdom, we must always proceed with the posture of a servant like Jesus. We must realize that authority and anointing flows from the top down. Just as the Psalmist declared in Psalm 133:2, "It is like precious oil poured on the head, running down on the beard, running down on Aaron's beard, down the collar of his robe," we will never have authority until we first live under authority. In a day and age where we often value title over testimony, prestige over purpose, and contract over covenant, this book is a holy call to understand honor, authority, and covering. Thank you, Gary, for writing a book that will not only extend the ministry life of the called, but also set in order the journey. Get this book! Live this book!

-Pat Schatzline

Evangelist, Author & CEO

Remnant Ministries International

I always considered myself someone who not only valued the principle of honor, but walked it out at a high-level. That was, until I met Gary Montoya. He has shown me ways to honor my leaders in habits I had never dreamed about. Gary has taught me the power behind the smallest of gestures and the beauty of consistent appreciation and love for those you serve. When it comes to honor, the only ones who should be writing about this topic, are people who live it every day of their life. Gary is one of those rare human beings. Whether you are a Pastor, ministry leader, or simply someone who wants to grow in this area, if you apply what you are about to read in Kingdom Honor, the only option is for Heaven to be opened up over your life, because God honors honor. Go through it with your team, or soak it all up on your own. Either way, it's not a stretch to say your life is about to change.

-Toby Bowker

Campus Pastor of The House San Diego

Pastor Gary Montoya lives and models what he has written. Every person who professes to love God regardless of their color, culture, title, position, gifting, or salary needs to read this book. The message in this book is vital if you are going to live heaven here on earth or be a child of God with power to live different from the world. I believe Kingdom Honor is a Spirit led message from God of what it means to love and serve God while serving people. Pastor Gary has captured this verse in his life and this book:

"There is no greater love than to lay down one's life
for one's friends." (John 15:13)

Kingdom Honor reveals how to live a successful blessed life by choosing to serve with a servant's heart through the Kingdom principles of honor. This is what builds great churches, leaders, and communities. This is where servants of God become Kings and Queens because we serve one another with honor and love like Jesus has loved us!

-Reverend Darwin Benjamin
Truth Ministries

KINGDOM HONOR
PUBLISHED BY Gary J. Montoya II

Edited by Elizabeth Allen

KINGDOM HONOR

HONOR

12 KEYS TO SERVING YOUR LEADERS AND UNLOCKING YOUR DESTINY

GARY MONTOYA

DEDICATION

I dedicate this book to Pastor Glen Berteau:

You have been my Pastor since I was 24 years old and brought me on staff to be your personal assistant when I was 28. For the last seven years, it has been an honor to travel with you on various outreach trips and serve with you in everyday ministry. The memories are priceless. You believed in me, taught me what it means to lead as Christ calls us, and have stretched me to develop into the leader that I am today. You saw things in me that I didn't see in myself. You have challenged me, corrected me, and encouraged me through the years. You have been there for Raquel and I in the most difficult times and have prayed us through every situation. Thank you from the bottom of my heart.

We love and honor you, today and forever.

SPECIAL THANKS

I want to give honor where honor is due:

Raquel Montoya: This book is complete because of you, I could not have finished this project without you. Thank you for hours upon hours of reading, reviewing and editing. I apologize for the constant going back and forth just to make one more last change. I am so grateful you are my wife and that we get to spend the rest of our lives together fulfilling God's call on our lives. What an adventure and a dream come true!

Pastor Toby Bowker: This book exists because you asked me to speak to your team in 2017. I never thought I would teach on the subject of honor, let alone write on the subject. That teaching turned into this book. It has been an honor speaking to your teams over the last few years. It has been a tremendous blessing to know you and do ministry with you!

John Bevere: I have considered you a spiritual father in my life since I was 18 years old. Your messages and books have inspired and challenged me to understand and value authority. This book was birthed out of the seeds you have sown. Your teachings have given me a hunger for more of God's Presence and the fear of the Lord in my life. It has been my honor to get to know you over the years. The times you have prayed for me and poured into me have impacted me greatly. This book would not have been written without the influence you have had in my life. Thank you for everything.

CONTENTS

SECTION 5 | RECOGNIZING REBELLION - PART 1

SECTION 6 | RECOGNIZING REBELLION - PART 2

SECTION 7 | FULFILLING YOUR GOD-GIVEN DREAM

FOREWORD

Gary Montoya has been my personal assistant for many years. He has traveled with me around the world and has had the opportunity to engage with some of the greatest pastors and ministries on the planet. Writing a book about honor and service requires a life actively lived in honor and service. Every chapter you read, Gary has lived.

Kingdom Honor is not another book to place on the shelf but a biblical mandate that will teach you how to honor and serve your leader God's way. This book is a must read for all those serving in ministry, whether they are volunteers, staff, or pastors. Christian men and women in the workplace will see their lives transformed by learning how to honor their secular leaders with Kingdom Honor. I am very excited about the powerful message presented in this book. I can honestly say, Gary has walked every principle written on these pages in serving and honoring me. He is a man of integrity and a special friend.

-Glen Berteau
Global Pastor, The House Network of Churches

INTRODUCTION

I never thought I would write a book on the subject of honor. It wasn't until January 2017 when the men's pastor at my church invited me to speak to his entire leadership team that the idea was first laid on my heart. He said, "Gary, I have watched the way you serve our Pastor the last few years and how you honor him. Can you teach my team about honor?" I gladly accepted the invitation. He really had no idea what I was going to share with them because I had no idea what I was going to share with them. I spent the next month praying and God began to reveal the message to me. It was the message I had been living and it was as if a light bulb had been turned on and illuminated what God had been building in my life. I finally was able to see that I had a passion and dedication to honor.

By that point in my life, I had served in multiple ministries for twelve years; everything from youth ministry, internships, international travel, evangelism, co-leading a men's small group, to overseeing communications and production teams. During the last seven years, my primary function has been assisting the Senior Pastor. Comprehending God's standard of honor came at the hefty price of me eating a lot of humble pie over the years. I made mistakes…big mistakes. I also made changes that altered my life for the better. But these events impacted me significantly, because each one showed that I was growing and learning this sacrificial life of honor. When the men's pastor asked me to share with his leaders, God showed me how He had developed honor in my life, and that He had a bigger purpose for that humble pie than I had originally believed.

When the time came to speak, I spent 50 minutes pouring into the men's team. Since then, that pastor has reached out to me multiple times telling me the massive impact the teaching had on his entire ministry, shifting the culture of his team. The impact that the honor principles had on the team spread quickly. I was asked to speak to other ministry teams at our church and I realized the body of Christ needed this message. The desire to share what God had revealed to me was born, teaching believers everywhere the power of serving your church and serving your leaders.

Many Christians are not walking in their calling or operating in their gifting because they are not planted and faithfully attending a local church. Serving is the key to discovering God's calling on your life. My prayer is that as you continue this book, your eyes will be opened to the truth of what it means to be a vessel of honor. I invite you to join the adventure and the journey. It is my hope that this book will inspire, equip, and motivate you to leave a legacy of honor.

Let your journey of honor begin!
- Gary

WHY THE CHURCH

SECTION 1

TIME TO BRING
HONOR BACK

Kingdom Honor is a powerful principle that produces multiplied effectiveness in the lives of believers who faithfully apply honor in every area of their lives. The principle of honoring will bring multiplication to your life wherever you apply it. If you give honor to your marriage, your marriage will become unbreakable and reach greater heights of intimacy and unity. If you show honor to your children, valuing them by spending quality time with them, training them, and being a godly example, your kids will grow into kingdom warriors. If you implement honor at your workplace, you will experience promotion, increase, job security, and supernatural influence. If you apply honor at your church, your gifting will have an eternal impact and your calling will come to fruition. The list goes on and on.

The meaning of the word honor[1] is to esteem, elevate, and hold someone in high regard and high value. When we honor the leaders that God has placed in our lives, we walk in true humility. When we humble ourselves, God gives us the grace needed to fulfill our callings. For us to effectively serve our leaders, God wants to refine and mold us into who we were created to be. The humble are those who God promotes. Unfortunately, most Christians do not understand what honor truly is or how important it is in The Kingdom of God.

In today's culture, we are seeing a tremendous lack of honor, particularly towards those in all manners of secular authority. Likewise, the sad truth is we also are seeing dishonor toward church leadership. As Christians, we are instructed to honor our church leaders, valuing them with great respect. It is a mandate for Christians.

"Honor those who are your leaders in the Lord's work."
(1 Thessalonians 5:12)

Though not always recognized as such, the local church is a Kingdom—a Kingdom that is an authority with order and structure. Yet, some people treat church like a social club or think of it as a Sunday hangout spot. Satan wants Christianity to become a culture that devalues the local church and its leaders. His goal is to ultimately tear down the Kingdom of God. In these last days, ministry is becoming more difficult for leaders. Here are some startling statistics on ministry leaders[2]:

- 57% can't pay their bills
- 54% of ministry leaders are overworked
- 43% are overstressed
- 34% battle discouragement
- 26% are overly fatigued
- 24% have a difficult time recruiting volunteers

These statistics provide insight into the culture of the body of Christ and explain why many churches are closing their doors and ministry leaders are throwing in the towel. One of the biggest burdens God has placed on me is to see the local church strengthened, and for that to happen, its leaders must be strengthened.

I have served as my Pastor's personal assistant for many years and have seen the positive impact honor has made not only on him but also on his ministry. I have also served as a ministry leader and can attest to the fact that leaders need members of the body to come alongside them to help fulfill the vision God has for their ministry. You and I can make a significant impact on our cities and churches by serving the leaders God has placed in our lives with honor. Just as Aaron and Hur held up Moses' arms during battle when he was exhausted, we must hold up our leader's arms. We must lighten the load, come alongside them, and help carry their burden.

When the church honors its leaders and serves the vision of the pastor, there will be unity, and it is here where God commanded His blessing (see Psalm 133). When that blessing is on a church or ministry team, the members of that church become unstoppable in their communities. Remember, honor is the key to multiplication, that exponential increase of effectiveness in ministry, and in the blessings of God within our lives.

WHAT IS KINGDOM HONOR?

As you begin to walk in your rightful position as a child of God, it is important that you and I understand the Kingdom of God and its authority. If we do not understand the authority of God's Kingdom, it will be difficult to apply the principles of honor in our lives. It can not be compared to the United States, which is the culture I have been raised in. Jesus said, "Your kingdom come, your will be done, on earth as it is in heaven" (Matthew 6:10 ESV). John tells us to, "Repent... for the kingdom of heaven is near" (Matthew 3:2). This Kingdom they spoke of is the kingdom you and I are a part of.

The Greek word for Kingdom is basileia[3]
Kingdom: royal power, kingship, dominion, rule of Jesus

The Kingdom of God is just that, a Kingdom. There is rank, rule, and order. God the Father, who is the head of Christ, has appointed His Son as the head over all rule and authority. Read the following scriptures in the New American Standard Bible to understand the scope of Jesus' authority.

- "For this reason also, God highly exalted Him, and bestowed on Him the name which is above every name." (Philippians 2:9)

- "He is also head of the body, the church; and He is the beginning, the firstborn from the dead, so that He Himself will come to have first place in everything." (Colossians 1:18)
- "He is the head over all rule and authority." (Colossians 2:10)
- "He is Lord of lords and King of kings." (Revelation 17:14)

The whole infrastructure of the Kingdom of God is built upon honor. As a matter of fact, God, "has given the Son absolute authority to judge, so that everyone will honor the Son, just as they honor the Father. Anyone who does not honor the Son is certainly not honoring the Father who sent him" (John 5:22-23). Honor is to be our culture and our identity. Peter instructs us to, "Honor all people, love the brotherhood, fear God, honor the king" (1 Peter 2:17 NASB).

Consider the very definition of this Biblical word – honor. Its core meaning comes from the Greek word timē[1]:

- A valuing by which the price is fixed
- To elevate and esteem (especially of the highest degree)
- To reverence

Other definitions[4]:
- To hold in honor and high respect
- To regard or treat (someone) with admiration or respect

Peter is saying that we are to esteem, elevate, and hold everyone in high regard and high value. The term all people refers to believers and non-believers. This may be shocking, but yes, we are commanded to honor every single person. You can see the honor principle is 360 degrees. Honor is to be shown to everyone of all backgrounds, age groups, ethnicities, and levels of authority. We are to have a deep value and appreciation for people whom God created in His image.

STEP INTO YOUR CALLING

Honor is the Path to Fulfilling God's Plans

There has never been a more urgent time in history for every believer to step into their calling and thrive. God has placed unique gifts inside each believer to fulfill a divine mandate from heaven. Similarly, we have designed and produced objects for our purposes. For example: a cell phone, car, airplane, or computer each has a specific purpose. Each invention we create is to help us accomplish things we desire to achieve or obtain. God is no different, and He has created you and me with a specific purpose to accomplish His desires on the earth.

The reality is, far too many Christians are not accomplishing their God-given dreams and living far below their potential. I used to work at a Fortune 500 company with employees that had college degrees and dreams that had no correlation to their current employment. Several times in casual conversation I would ask, "Why are you here?" and the answer was always the same, "I need to pay my bills." Deep down this answer always bothered me. I had this check in my spirit because these were good people who had never tapped into their God-given gifts or calling. These were people who never experienced the grace of thriving in their uniqueness for Him. They didn't understand that honor was the key to unlocking the plans God had for them.

In my experience, you can categorize Christians into three groups:

Group One: They love God, but they are not in their assignment nor calling.

Group Two: They love God. They are in their assignment and calling, but they are not thriving in their calling.

Group Three: They love God. They are in their area of assignment, and they are thriving and multiplying.

Which category do you fall into? Be encouraged that life's successes are not measured by how you start your race but how you finish it. None of us started right, we were all born into sin. But we all can choose how we finish. As you begin this journey of Kingdom Honor you will see God do the miraculous in your life. God will refine you like gold: removing the impurities and developing a servant's heart in you.

THE PROMISE

> "Now in a great house there are not only vessels of gold and silver but also of wood and clay, some for honorable use, some for dishonorable. Therefore, if anyone cleanses himself from what is dishonorable, he will be a vessel for honorable use, set apart as holy, useful to the master of the house, ready for every good work."
> (2 Timothy 2:20-21 ESV)

This verse is one of the most remarkable promises in the Bible. Paul says if you cleanse yourself from dishonor, you will be restored as a vessel of honor. It is God's original design for you to be a vessel of honor. Do you want to be a vessel of honor - set apart and useful for the Master? Do you want to be prepared for the work He has assigned for you? Here is the astounding truth, the choice is yours. It is 100% God's will for you to bear much fruit and to multiply in every area of your life. You were designed to thrive in your calling. This pleases God! Jesus said, "My Father is glorified by this, that you bear much fruit, and so prove to be My disciples" (John 15:8 NASB). It is clear how God wants you to finish. Jesus also said,

> "I am the true grapevine, and my Father is the gardener. He cuts off every branch of mine that doesn't produce fruit, and he prunes the branches that do bear fruit so they will produce even more."
> (John 15:1-2)

He cuts off every branch that doesn't bear fruit, but the good news is that God "prunes the branches that do bear fruit so that you will produce even more"! You are to bear fruit at an accelerated rate. Do you feel you have made mistakes that are irreparable or feel you waited too long to fulfill your calling? Maybe you are not where you should be? If you feel delayed in any way, be encouraged - hold tight to this promise:

> "You will restore me to even greater honor and comfort me once again." (Psalm 71:21)

David declared this over his life, though he had committed adultery and was responsible for the murder of an innocent man. He repented and declared this promise over his life. You and I need to do the same. This is a remarkable promise, settle in your heart now that no matter what is in your past, God will restore you to even greater honor. My wife has said, "Restoration is the signature of God's divine nature."

This is what God does best:
He restores, heals, and makes new.

When you first got saved, God planted dreams in your heart. He intended to give you glimpses of your future. Even though you may feel you have missed your calling or have been delayed, God can and will renew you. He takes a shattered dream and creates a new one. He restores what the enemy has stolen. If you focus on becoming a vessel of honor, nothing and no one can stop you from fulfilling your calling.

Lord, I thank you for the opportunity to start fresh in my life. So many times, I have missed the mark. I am sorry Lord. Forgive me for having dishonor in my heart. I choose today to move beyond my past mistakes to declare I am wholly yours to refine. Help me cleanse myself with your Word to become a vessel of honor. In Jesus' name, amen.

THE IMPACT OF DISHONOR

Most people do not realize the magnitude of honor nor the repercussions of dishonor. Dishonor cripples you in every area of your life. Dishonor invades your prayer life, your family, your church and your workplace.

DISHONOR HINDERS ANSWERED PRAYER

Let's further examine the magnitude of dishonor by using an illustration between husbands and wives,

> "In the same way, you husbands must give honor to your wives. Treat your wife with understanding as you live together. She may be weaker than you are, but she is your equal partner in God's gift of new life. Treat her as you should so your prayers will not be hindered." (1 Peter 3:7)

The key to this verse is honor. Paul tells husbands they must give honor—not as an option, but as a command. The man is to esteem his wife, highly elevating and valuing her. When he withholds honor from her, his prayers are hindered. Hindered prayers are damaging not only to the husband but to the entire family. Remember, she is God's daughter that has been entrusted to the husband. Husbands are the head of the wife

(Ephesians 5:23) and will be held accountable for how he treats her, cares for her, and cultivates her. This reality is sobering and should cause men to walk in the fear of the Lord, valuing their wives with the utmost respect. Husbands are commanded in Ephesians 5:25-26 to:

- Love their wives as Christ loves the church
- Give up their life for her
- Make her holy and clean by the washing of God's Word

Your prayers will be hindered due to dishonor. The Greek definition for the word hindered is "to cut off"[1]. Have you ever had your phone service cut off? That is what happens to prayers when dishonor is in one's heart, the direct line to God is "cut off". If you are cut off, you are not going to receive any kind of miracles or answered prayers. How many men have gone years with their prayers being hindered because of withholding honor from their wives? Nothing, according to scripture, so clearly affects your prayer life as honor does.

I notice my prayer life elevates dramatically when I honor my wife. As a matter of fact, without exaggeration, I hear from God the fastest and most concretely when I am praying seeking to honor my wife. I could be seeking the Lord concerning ministry endeavors, daily guidance, or any need I may have; but the moment I pray about honoring my wife, the answer comes swiftly every single time.

I now often ask, "How can I honor my wife?" Almost immediately the Holy Spirit will tell me, "help her with that project, vacuum the house, do the dishes, take her on a date, send her a message, help her at work, get her a gift, etc." The answers come quickly and specifically. If you are married, try it! Simply ask, "How can I honor my spouse today?" Watch how quickly the Holy Spirit will speak to you, and then be obedient. I can see how my honor causes ripple effects in my marriage. Honoring literally invigorates the very core of my wife's being. It's as if the honor I am sowing into her develops into unity between us and confidence in herself. Our relationship is fortified because of the trust honor cultivates.

One day while praying, "How can I honor my wife?" I was led to clean the house: vacuuming, laundry, cleaning the bathroom, and dishes. I am ashamed to say that for the first eight years of my marriage, I only did these tasks a handful of times. As I was completing these tasks, I genuinely asked the Lord to change my heart towards cleaning the house. When you sincerely ask God to change your heart and give Him full access, He does just that. God moved in me quickly and I began assisting with these tasks more than I ever had before. And to my surprise, what I hated doing before, I now enjoy. Through honoring my wife, my prayers were unhindered, and God answered me quickly!

Dishonor will cut off your direct line to God.
Honor will give you direct access to God.

DISHONOR SHUTS THE DOORWAY TO MIRACLES

In the book of Mark, we learn about one of the most interesting accounts of Jesus when He returned to His hometown. It is perplexing because it says, "He couldn't do any miracles," (6:5 NLT). Yes, you read that correctly, He could not do miracles! This shocked me, compelling me to research further, and to my discovery, every translation presents the same situation. Here are a few of the translations:

> "He could do no mighty work there." (ESV)
> "He could not do a miracle there at all." (AMP)
> "So Jesus was not able to work any miracles." (NCV)

Can you see why this is mind-blowing? Jesus is a miracle worker, and yet in this account, He was not able to perform the miracles He desired to do. Let's read the situation in its entirety to grasp the impact of Honor:

"Jesus left that part of the country and returned with his disciples to Nazareth, his hometown. The next Sabbath he began teaching in the synagogue, and many who heard him were amazed. They asked, 'Where did he get all this wisdom and the power to perform such miracles?' Then they scoffed, 'He's just a carpenter, the son of Mary and the brother of James, Joseph, Judas, and Simon. And his sisters live right here among us.' They were deeply offended and refused to believe in him. Then Jesus told them, 'A prophet is honored everywhere except in his own hometown and among his relatives and his own family.' And because of their unbelief, he couldn't do any miracles among them except to place his hands on a few sick people and heal them. And he was amazed at their unbelief." (Mark 6:1-6)

The people were astonished by his teaching; His wisdom and revelation were remarkable. They took note that Jesus spoke with authority, they heard about the miracles He had performed at other cities yet they themselves were unable to experience His miraculous power.

The passage does not say, "He wouldn't do miracles"; it says, "He couldn't". The question arises, "Why couldn't Jesus do mighty miracles for them?" Scripture indicates that acts of healing are different from performing miracles (1 Corinthians 12:9-10). Jesus was able to heal a few people but not able to perform miracles. At first glance, I thought it was because of their unbelief or because they were offended. Both are true, however, when Jesus addressed them, He didn't mention their offense or lack of faith but instead exposed the root issue in verse four.

He told them, "A prophet is honored everywhere except in his own hometown and among his relatives and his own family." Their lack of honor hindered them from receiving miracles from Jesus.

Dishonor shuts the door on miracles.
Honor opens the door for miracles.

DISHONOR DESTROYS THE BODY

Unfortunately, dishonor is as prevalent in the church today as it was with the church of Corinth. The Corinthian church brought judgement on themselves with their dishonor towards one another. Paul addresses the church of Corinth and tells them,

> "For it sounds as if more harm than good is done when you meet together. First, I hear that there are divisions among you when you meet as a church, and to some extent I believe it. But, of course, there must be divisions among you so that you who have God's approval will be recognized! When you meet together, you are not really interested in the Lord's Supper. For some of you hurry to eat your own meal without sharing with others. As a result, some go hungry while others get drunk. What? Don't you have your own homes for eating and drinking? Or do you really want to disgrace God's church and shame the poor? What am I supposed to say? Do you want me to praise you? Well, I certainly will not praise you for this!" (1 Corinthians 11:17-22)

The body was not in unity nor were they honoring one another while partaking in communion. In actuality, they were humiliating the poor by simply not waiting for each other to eat. Paul goes on to say, "So, my dear brothers and sisters, when you gather for the Lord's Supper, wait for each other. If you are really hungry, eat at home so you won't bring judgment upon yourselves when you meet together," (v33, 34).

I was shocked when I first read this scripture. Who would have thought not waiting for other believers during communion would bring judgement? By rushing to eat they exposed the root issue of dishonor. When they refused to wait for others to take communion, the believers were esteeming themselves above their brothers and sisters. This is a dishonor not only to the body but to Jesus himself. Paul warns us,

"That is why you should examine yourself before eating the bread and drinking the cup. For if you eat the bread or drink the cup without honoring the body of Christ, you are eating and drinking God's judgment upon yourself. That is why many of you are weak and sick, and some have even died." (1 Corinthians 11:28-30)

Some people believe they can honor Jesus but dishonor other believers. This is a dangerous mindset to have. Their disregard for other members of the church resulted in communion being taken in an unworthy manner (v27), which led to judgement in their lives. Paul tells us the consequence of their dishonor was believers experiencing weakness, sickness, and even death! The first word Paul mentions is weak, without strength. An absence of honor equals an absence of strength. Dishonoring people will make you weak.

DISHONOR DILUTES YOUR LOVE OF GOD

The way you honor people is the way you honor God. We are told, "If someone says, "I love God," but hates a fellow believer, that person is a liar; for if we don't love people we can see, how can we love God, whom we cannot see?" (1 John 4:20).

If you want to know how much you love God, ask yourself,
Who is the person that you love the least?

This is a direct question, be prepared for God to bring a direct answer. Allow the Holy Spirit to show you those you love the least and then ask Him for a greater measure of love for them. Seek to value them the same way Jesus does. If you are sincere in your prayer, God will answer your prayers and begin to change your heart. As your love for people grows, you will be amazed at how you personally are transformed.

The depth of your walk with God is directly correlated with your love and honor for others.

THE IMPACT OF HONOR

Just as dishonor wreaks havoc in the life of a believer, honor creates peace, fulfillment, and multiplication in the life of a believer.

HONOR IS THE PATH TO HEAVEN

In Matthew 25, Jesus addresses two groups of people. The first group He welcomed into the kingdom of Heaven, simply because they treated people as if they were Jesus Himself. The second group of people Jesus sentenced to hell, and they were shocked. Jesus' response to the second group was, "When you refused to help the least of these my brothers and sisters, you were refusing to help me" (Matthew 25:45).

Why were these people sentenced to hell? One word: dishonor. They did not honor the least. They did not value or esteem them, therefore they did not honor God. The Bible puts great emphasis on valuing those whom society deems as insignificant or unimportant. When we honor them, we honor God.

"Those who oppress the poor insult their Maker, but helping the poor honors him." (Proverbs 14:31)

I want to challenge you to always look for the need in other's lives. The next time you see someone homeless or hungry, think of them as Jesus Himself. Help them find shelter or buy them a meal. The next time you see someone poorly clothed, give them some of your clothes or take them shopping. If you know someone in prison or juvenile hall, go visit them. Many of them have lost all hope and feel forgotten by the world. Whatever the need is, meet the need and take care of them like you would if it was Jesus standing before you. You and I are not called to help the entire world, but we are called to help those who God brings across our paths.

> "If you help the poor, you are lending to the Lord and he will repay you!" (Proverbs 19:17)

HONOR PROMISES SUCCESS AND PROLONGED LIFE

> "Honor your father and mother." This is the first commandment with a promise: If you honor your father and mother, "things will go well for you, and you will have a long life on the earth." (Ephesians 6:2-3)

This is the first commandment God ever gave mankind with a promise. Consider how remarkable this is: You and I have a guaranteed promise that things will go well for us if we choose to simply honor our parents. Our biological fathers and mothers are God's authority in our lives from birth, and we are to obey them until we are married. When you get married, you are no longer under their authority, as explained in Matthew 19:5, when a man leaves his father and mother and is joined to his wife, the two are united into one. This means that those who are married will leave from under the authority of their parents and join their spouse so that God can establish a new family authority. After marriage, we are called to still honor our parents. I cannot tell you how many times I have had success after honoring my parents, even when I couldn't see the immediate benefit of it.

When you honor your father and mother, you will live a long life- a life full of faith and God's power moving through you. I know this is easy to do when someone has good or godly parents. Where the challenge lies is when parents are not loving, caring, responsible for providing or protecting their children. Neglect can come in many shapes and the truth is no parent is ever perfect. However, I want to challenge you to still honor them even in these situations, as your honor will speak volumes to them. Your life will radiate, and your parents will see God in you and through you. Death and life are in the power of your words, speak life to your parents. Tell them you love them often, tell them you respect them, try to honor them with your words and actions, and let God do the rest.

I want to mention that if someone is in a physically or sexually abusive home, honoring your parents does not mean you have to allow them to abuse you. Seek help from the authorities (pastors, teachers, police department, etc.) Those parents are breaking the law. You can love and honor your parents without being in the same home if there is abuse.

This promise of blessing definitely applies to honoring our physical parents, but it goes much further and deeper, extending to our spiritual parents as well. The relationship of a spiritual son and father is unique, many times surpassing that of flesh and blood. On one occasion, Jesus was teaching in a house and His mother Mary came to the door looking for Him. Someone yelled to Jesus, "Your Mother and brothers are at the door." And Jesus' responded, "My mother and my brothers are all those who hear God's word and obey it" (Luke 8:21). Jesus was making it crystal clear that spiritual DNA transcends physical DNA. It is one thing to be family by blood, but another thing to be family in spirit. One family unit is temporal, the other is eternal.

Paul himself was a spiritual father, he said to the Corinthian church, "…I became your father in Christ Jesus when I preached the Good News to you" (1 Corinthians 4:15). Other times he mentions his spiritual sons Timothy and Onesimus (1 Timothy 1:2, Philemon 1:10).

Who are your fathers and mothers in the faith? Who are your spiritual leaders? If you apply the kingdom principle of honor to them, things will go well for you and you will be successful in your calling. This is a promise you can invest your whole life in because it's guaranteed from God the Father Himself.

HONOR PROTECTS YOU FROM POVERTY

It is not God's will for His children to suffer poverty. Although God does not desire for any of His children to be in poverty or need, we sometimes encounter circumstances in which we are subjected to financial crises. Even through those times, God promises to provide for our needs if we honor Him. Our Father promises His children that we will never lack (Psalm 23:1, Philippians 4:19). Even the children of Israel while in the wilderness had all of their needs met. One of the main ways God desires us to honor Him is in the area of our finances, yet this tends to be one of the most difficult areas to conquer for most people. God promises that if we honor Him with our income, multiplication will be amplified in our lives. Look at what Proverbs says:

> "Honor the Lord with your wealth and with the first and best part of all your income. Then your barns will be full, and your vats will overflow with fresh wine." (Proverbs 3:9-10 GOD'S WORD)

One of the main ways we honor God is by financially supporting the local church. See what Paul says to those who honor God with their finances:

> "God will generously provide all you need. Then you will always have everything you need and plenty left over to share with others… For God is the one who provides seed for the farmer and

then bread to eat. In the same way, he will provide and increase your resources and then produce a great harvest of generosity in you. Yes, you will be enriched in every way so that you can always be generous." (2 Corinthians 9:8, 10-11)

Honoring God with your finances will ensure you have plenty left over to share with others and enable you to be generous. God wants you to always be generous so you can help meet the needs of the church and support the work of various ministries. I know giving is a struggle for a lot of people, because the questions always come up, "what about my house, and what about my bills?" When you put God first in this area, God takes care of the rest (Matthew 6:33).

HONOR MAKES YOU ATTRACTIVE

We already know God is attractive in every way, but the world doesn't know this. They are entirely blind. They have never met God. Here is the good news- they have met you! Here is the bad news- they have met you! This is laughable but true. Have you ever thought that you are the only Bible some people will ever read? You are a child of God, you reflect Him. Did you ever think that you could make God and His Word attractive?

> "Slaves must always obey their masters and do their best to please them. They must not talk back or steal, but must show themselves to be entirely trustworthy and good. Then they will make the teaching about God our Savior attractive in every way." (Titus 2:9-10)

When we are honorable, people of integrity, we make the gospel attractive to others. We have the ability to display His beauty on earth. He is awe-inspiring and He is Wonderful (Isaiah 9:6), but the world doesn't know Him, they know us. It brings a whole new meaning to what Jesus said, "Anyone who has seen me has seen the Father!"(John 14:9). Can you say that about yourself? If people see you, have they seen God? Peter addresses the attractiveness of honor when speaking to wives in 1 Peter:

> "In the same way, you wives must accept the authority of your husbands. Then, even if some refuse to obey the Good News, your godly lives will speak to them without any words. They will be won over by observing your pure and reverent lives… This is how the holy women of old made themselves beautiful. They put their trust in God and accepted the authoity of their husbands."
> (1 Peter 3:1-2, 5)

Peter is saying that the reason holy women are beautiful is that they trust God and honor their husband's authority. They aren't doormats who are trampled on, but they honor the God-ordained leadership that God has given husbands. It is through honor and their godly lives that the message of the gospel is spoken. Our godly lives will speak louder than words ever could. We are still called to preach the gospel to the nations, but we also want to "win people over by our pure and reverent lives." Unbelievers have seen the world's beauty, which is skin deep and fades quickly. However, when they meet believers who are Christ-like, they will be attracted to them and want to know more about what sets them apart.

Honor allows Christ's beauty to radiate through us.

THE IMPORTANCE OF CHURCH AUTHORITY

It is our job as the church to set the example and bring honor to our homes, our churches, and our lives. It all begins with the Church. But before we can understand how to honor our church authority it is important to make it clear why we must honor them. There are many believers who do not value or respect ministry leaders like they do other positions of authority. Far too many believers make it obvious through their actions that they honor themselves above the church and its God-ordained authority. People would never be late to work or skip it whenever they don't feel like showing up, yet don't mind being late to Church and many stay home whenever the mood strikes them. Even though the pastor puts his heart and soul into preparing a weekly message for them, they have a casual attitude about it and don't really appreciate it. Some sit in service checking their social media and texts, responding to those messages, yet not responding to God's message.

Far too many believers spend the service checked out instead of checking their hearts.

We need to understand that passion for God's house consumed Jesus! (see John 2:17). If Jesus is passionate about the church, we should be passionate about the church. Not only did Jesus start the church, but He also established and organized church leadership for you and I.

Ephesians 4:11-13 is very clear:

> "Now these are the gifts Christ gave to the church: the apostles, the prophets, the evangelists, and the pastors and teachers. Their responsibility is to equip God's people to do his work and build up the church, the body of Christ. This will continue until we all come to such unity in our faith."

Jesus empowered church leadership with the responsibility to equip us for the work of ministry with the very purpose of building the church. God has placed spiritual gifts inside you, and you are called to walk in that gifting and calling to impact this world and your generation. Paul tells us,

> "In his grace, God has given us different gifts for doing certain things well." (Romans 12:6)

Those gifts are what will set you apart and give you that edge in life to advance the Kingdom. We as believers only flourish when we are planted in the House of God (Psalm 92:13). The role church leaders play in the Body's life is to equip the saints and spiritually strengthen them. We all need church leadership in our lives to correct, rebuke, and disciple us with the goal of training us for the ministry. If we do not honor and esteem our church leaders, how can we expect them to be able to fulfill their role effectively? If they are unable to train us effectively, how can we possibly have multiplied effectiveness for Jesus in our lives?

We all need each other; not one-part of the Church functions correctly on its own. We belong to each other. You need me and I need you. Try to imagine if all your body parts had their own agenda. If you literally had no control of your body, you would be crippled and disabled. This is what believers look like when they are not in unity with the body of Christ and when they disconnect themselves from the local church.

On the other hand, I have also seen people attend a church that never thrives. The reason is that they are not serving to help build up the church, they just sit in the pew. This was one of the issues Paul had to address, because some Christians were idle, lazy and became busy bodies not serving or helping to build the church.

When we dishonor our God-given authority through lack of submission and service, we limit our ability to prosper the way God longs for. Until you have submitted to authority, God will not give you the authority you need to fulfill your calling. You have to submit to authority to be trusted with authority. David had to serve Saul before he could ever be king. We are a part of a Kingdom that is greater than ourselves. Accept it as truth and be liberated in your calling.

"Everyone must submit to governing authorities. For all authority comes from God, and those in positions of authority have been placed there by God. So anyone who rebels against authority is rebelling against what God has instituted, and they will be punished. For the authorities do not strike fear in people who are doing right, but in those who are doing wrong. Would you like to live without fear of the authorities? Do what is right, and they will honor you." (Romans 13:1-3)

It is important to note that God designed the whole infrastructure of authority for the purpose of establishing order in our countries and churches. First, Paul refers to governing authorities such as presidents, governors and mayors. He then clarifies, "all authority comes from God." Whether it is government, family, school, business, or the church, God is the one who establishes authority. Paul explains a Kingdom principle here: when you do what is right, those in leadership "will honor you." What is the implication?

God will honor and promote you through those in authority.

ALL AUTHORITY IS APPOINTED

I know this concept of authority and honor goes against our flesh and carnal nature. Our flesh does not want to submit to anyone. The lifestyle of honor can be even more difficult to wrap our minds around when it comes to evil and corrupt political leaders. We question: "Did God appoint them?" Yes. The Bible clearly says that those in positions of authority have been placed there by God (Romans 13:1). A common follow-up question we ask is, "Why did He appoint them?" We must understand God put them in position because He has a plan. We see the plan of God from Genesis to Revelation. When you look at some of the worst leaders in history such as Pharaoh, King Saul, or Nebuchadnezzar, God used every one of them in their exact positions of authority.

> "The Scriptures say that God told Pharaoh, 'I have appointed you for the very purpose of displaying my power in you and to spread my fame throughout the earth.'" (Romans 9:17)

God appointed Pharaoh, who was one of the cruelest leaders to walk this earth. He killed thousands of babies and enslaved millions of people. Yet scripture says God appointed him for His purposes to display His power and to spread His fame throughout the earth. That is the purpose of the Gospel! This is a critical scripture we must remember when there is wicked and cruel leadership in position, to remind us, it is always for God's purposes.

Ellicott's Commentary states [1]:
> "Each ruler of the great empires of the world was, in ways he knew not, working out the purposes of God."

Geneva Study Bible states[2]:
> "So the wicked and Satan himself are God's servants, because he

makes them serve him by constraint and turns that which they do out of malice to his honor and glory."

No one gets in office or acquires a position of authority without God's knowledge or will. We are also told, "The Most High God rules over the kingdoms of the world and appoints anyone he desires to rule over them" (Daniel 5:21). God will even use wicked political leaders to bring about His plans. Praying for those in governmental leadership is a very important task assigned to us as believers.

> "Ask God to help them; intercede on their behalf, and give thanks
> for them. Pray this way for kings and all who are in authority."
> (1 Timothy 2:1-2)

It is very easy to gossip about political leaders, but that changes nothing except our hearts by corrupting them. Prayer changes everything.

THE TRAP OF LEAVING THE CHURCH

I have seen people leave churches due to an offense, often rooted in a refusal to submit to church authority, and they never thrive or flourish in their callings. Why? Their lack of honor created a stubborn, prideful attitude that removed them from the power of unity within the Body of Christ.

Far too many have fallen into the trap of leaving church or not attending as often as they should. Isolating believers is the goal of the enemy. When a sheep is isolated from the herd, it has no protection. Have you noticed that Christians fall into sin when they have no accountability? This is why we absolutely need each other.

When Christians abandon churches, not only do they lose their protection of accountability, but this also weakens the structure and foundation of the Body of Christ. The devil knows this all too well. There seems to be many Christians who think they don't need to go to church, this idea couldn't be further from the truth!

> "You should not stay away from the church meetings, as some are doing, but you should meet together and encourage each other. Do this even more as you see the day coming." (Hebrews 10:25 NCV)

It is apparent that people leaving churches became a problem in the early church and this is why it was addressed here. We are instructed not to miss church meetings even more now as it gets closer to the end. You may have heard it said before by professing Christians, "I don't need to go to church to be a Christian," or "I'm a Christian, but I don't like organized religion". We've all heard these excuses. The problem with these statements is that you never hear Peter, James, or Paul making statements like this. On the contrary, the entire New Testament is full of instructions for establishing the local church.

The early church fathers spent their lives building the local church and many gave their lives for it. They knew how important this mission was and what it meant to God to build the church. These leaders were led by the Holy Spirit to give us protocols for everything from order in church services, appointing leaders and pastors in cities, qualifications of elders and deacons, and receiving offerings. They instruct us on dealing with sin within the church, the administration of spiritual gifts, and even how to pray. The list goes on and on.

Scripture shows us that the early church and its members dove in with one focus and purpose to establish the church. They gave tremendous amounts of resources: time, finances, and abilities, freely to the church and its mission (Acts 2:42-45). Make it your aim to be as zealous about building God's House as the early church leaders were. God said, "Rebuild my house. Then I will take pleasure in it and be honored," (Haggai 1:8).

David said, "But I am like an olive tree, thriving in the house of God" (Psalm 52:8). Stay plugged into your church, stay faithful. The devil's agenda is to isolate you from your church, your pastor, your brothers, and sisters to devour you. Don't fall into his trap. Be on guard!

SECTION 1: SUMMARY

1) Honor is a powerful principle that produces multiplied effectiveness in the lives of believers who faithfully apply honor in every area of their lives.

2) Applying honor brings us closer to God in not only our prayer lives but opens the door to miracles and heaven itself. Honor brings us success, protects us, and makes us effective witnesses of the Gospel. Applying dishonor to our lives weakens us spiritually, mentally, and physically.

3) We are called to be in the church body, we cannot see effectiveness in our lives without being plugged into the Body of Christ. "You should not stay away from the church meetings, as some are doing, but you should meet together and encourage each other. Do this even more as you see the day coming" (Hebrews 10:25 NCV).

4) God has uniquely gifted each one of us to serve the Kingdom according to his purposes. Honoring our leaders brings powerful anointing to our giftedness. When we serve our leaders with honor, our gifts are activated, our ministries thrive, and the Kingdom of God is exponentially more effective!

SECTION 1: ACTION STEPS

1) Pray about a specific act of honor you can do for the following relationships this week.

    a. Spouse

    b. Parent

    c. Pastor/Spiritual Leader

    d. Boss

2) Are you plugged into the local church? If not, pray that God shows you which church in your city you should attend and serve at.

3) Talk with your spiritual leader or pastor about any distractions that are holding you back from serving to your full capacity.

Lord, I didn't understand how my ability to honor is directly connected to so many areas of my life. Cleanse my heart of dishonor and help me to supernaturally increase honoring the people you have surrounded me with. I want to live in the goodness that honor cultivates in my life but most importantly, I want to please you. In Jesus' name, amen.

HOW TO HONOR YOUR LEADERS - PART I

SECTION 2

KINGDOM KEY #1
BE A VESSEL OF
HONOR

Now that you understand why honor is so important in the life of a believer and why it is crucial that we honor our leaders, let's dive into the 12 Biblical Keys that will teach you to serve your leaders exceptionally well. This first key, Be a Vessel of Honor, is the Master Key upon which the rest of the keys are built on. Once this principle is established as a cornerstone in your life and you are doing the daily work to engrave it on your heart, you will see the fruit and rewards of honor in your life. Without it, you will be building on a faulty foundation full of cracks.

I have seen too many people try to bypass this principle, and it grieves my heart because many of them did not endure as a result of them neglecting this first Kingdom Key. On the other hand, I have seen those pursue God with everything and still not endure, simply because they did not guard their hearts.

When I was 18 years old, I joined a ministry internship. At the time, the internship was a part of the largest coalition of internships with over 5,000 interns nationwide. I was on a team of interns in Northern California for three years. Throughout that time, I served with 30-40 other interns in an intense program. We served and evangelized in churches, high school assemblies, and youth groups. We read through the Bible cover to cover, gathered for multiple weekly prayers sessions and participated in countless productions that illustrated the gospel. We attended three international mission trips to Peru, Africa, and the Philippines. We saw thousands of lost souls give their lives to Christ.

The heartbreaking reality is that today, half of those I served with are no longer in ministry. Some got pregnant out of wedlock. Others got married to other interns, who are now divorced. Some don't go to church anymore. Some of them don't even believe in God anymore and are now professing Atheists.

How does this happen? We were seeing multitudes of people getting saved everywhere we went! Our team was led by godly pastors. How did these ministry leaders, interns or staff members fall away from Jesus? This was not only a problem with our team, but a world-wide epidemic that spans all denominations, ministries, and ages. If you have done ministry for any length of time, you probably know people who are no longer serving the church and or have even forfeited their faith. Jesus actually prophesied this was going to happen to Christians in the Last Days. He said, "Many will turn away from me ... and the love of many will grow cold. But the one who endures to the end will be saved." (Matthew 24:10-13) God does not want you to start the race to only get burnt out on ministry and ultimately lose your love for Him. It is God's desire that you endure to the end and finish the race He has set before you!

HOLINESS STILL MATTERS

"Therefore, if anyone cleanses himself from what is dishonorable, he will be a vessel for honorable use, set apart as holy, useful to the master of the house, ready for every good work." (2 Timothy 2:21 ESV)

Of all the verses that explain becoming honorable, this verse summarizes it best! Paul tells us that if we desire to serve God, our church and leaders exceptionally, we must cleanse ourselves from everything that is dishonorable in our lives. It is then and only then that we will be honorable vessels, set apart and holy, ready and useful to fulfill God's call on our lives. There are no shortcuts or exceptions to this principle.

> The word holy[1] used in this verse means to be sanctified: to separate from profane things and dedicate to God.

The word holy is not a popular word in today's culture, but it is greatly admired and esteemed in the Kingdom. Those that are holy are the ones that God uses for extraordinary purposes. They have been set apart from worldliness and sin, consecrated and dedicated for His holy works. When one is set apart, there is a visible difference obvious to those around them. They are not one that is influenced by culture, rather they influence culture like a light in the darkness. It is His presence in their life that separates them. When God's presence is on you, His extraordinary ability is functioning in you. This is why the enemy has done everything in his power to get the church away from holiness.

When the church is holy, it becomes a weapon to defeat the powers of darkness.

Jesus gave His life for this purpose of making you holy and He is returning for a church that is nothing less than that (Ephesians 5:25-26). This is why we are instructed to actively, "Pursue peace with all people, and holiness, without which no one will see the Lord" (Hebrews 12:14 NKJV).

We are called to pursue holiness! The Greek word for pursuit is diōkō2 It is a passionate seeking; it is aggressive, intentional and eager. Does this define your pursuit of holiness? I pray that as you read this you are desiring to live a life more pleasing to Him than ever before. It is important to note that the moment you got saved you were made holy! Here's the good news! Holiness is not an action that you can achieve within your own power. It is God's power at work for you! "For God is working in you, giving you the desire and the power to do what pleases him" (Philippians 2:13). Notice how this process is a partnership with God. Now I need to make this point clear, when you got saved you became holy in your spirit (Colossians 1:22). Your spirit was renewed, and you were made right with God. This is justification – this is God's part. He made us right with God and set us free from the power of sin (Romans 6:22). However, we must pursue sanctification, this is holiness that is manifested from the inside out – this is our part and responsibility. This is where we cleanse ourselves.

"And everyone who has this hope fixed on Him purifies himself, just as He is pure." (1 John 3:3 NASB)

"Therefore, having these promises, beloved, let us cleanse ourselves from all defilement of flesh and spirit, perfecting holiness in the fear of God."(2 Corinthians 7:1 NASB)

"Let us also lay aside every weight, and sin which clings so closely, and let us run with endurance the race that is set before us." (Hebrews 12:1 ESV)

It is clearly our responsibility. This is where you prove by the way you live that you have repented of your sins and turned to God (Matthew 3:8). This is where it is evident to all around us that the work of salvation is in effect in our lives. Paul said, "We prove ourselves by our purity" (2 Corinthians 6:6).

GUARD YOUR HEART

"Guard your heart above all else, for it determines the course of your life." (Proverbs 4:23)

Anyone that has ever fallen away from the Lord, or have forfeited their calling, was not guarding their heart. We guard our homes with security systems, we lock our doors, our cars, so our vehicle and its valuables won't get stolen. We secure our money by putting it in banks where there are vaults and security guards. But God says above everything we are to guard our hearts. How much more valuable is your heart than a house, car, or money? Your heart is the command center of your life and determines the course it takes. Let's look at what guarding our hearts mean:

The Hebrew word for heart is Leb[3]: seat of appetites, seat of emotions and seat of passion. It is in the heart where affections are stored, that is why it needs to be guarded. The devil is always vying for our affections and the things we are most passionate about.

When we start loving things in this world, the love of God grows cold. The flame for God slowly dies out. Remember Jesus said to a church, "'But I have this complaint against you. You don't love me or each other as you did at first! Look how far you have fallen! Turn back to me and do the works you did at first. If you don't repent, I will come and remove your lampstand from its place among the churches'" (Revelation 2:4-5). So many of the interns I served with turned away from the Lord because their love grew cold. They failed to guard their hearts and it cost them their ministry and their intimacy with the Savior.

You have to be open and honest with yourself and ask who or what has your affections? This is why you have to examine yourself continually. You have to guard your affections constantly. A few years ago, my wife and I had gotten a streaming account and started to watch a top-rated show. We got hooked on watching this show daily. Some nights we would watch 2-3 episodes. However, the Holy Spirit checked us on it and convicted our hearts. He told me that this show had my affections, so we quit watching it. I was not spending quality time with God during that season, I was not waking up early to spend time with God because I was spending too much time watching that show late at night. Can you see how we can easily trade greater things for lesser things?

I thank God for showing me the error of my way and teaching me not to watch anything that hooks my affections. Don't get me wrong, we still watch shows and movies periodically. But we are cautious, and we set up parameters to ensure the content is clean, pure, and inspiring. The psalmist declared,

"I will refuse to look at anything vile and vulgar." (Psalm 101:3)

You have to be careful when you are choosing what entertainment you are going to allow into your home and your heart. You are the temple of the Holy Spirit and are commanded not to grieve Him (Ephesians 4:30). This is why we are to guard our hearts; to guard our relationship with the Holy Spirit. If you want a strong relationship with Him, which I hope you do, protect your relationship. Don't participate in anything that grieves the Holy Spirit. If you cultivate an atmosphere that honors Him, you will have a strong relationship with Him, and He will honor you with His presence.

"I will honor those who honor me, and I will despise those that think lightly of me." (1 Samuel 2:30)

A youth leader invited me to lunch recently and expressed that he was struggling with being on fire for God. The Holy Spirit prompted me to question the kind of music he was listening to. Right away it was like a light bulb went off and he was convicted. He was listening to music that was promoting sexuality, violence, and had foul language. My heart broke as I found out some of the other youth leaders were partaking in worldliness too. He then humbly asked, "Where do we draw the line?" I told him, "As a child of God, if it promotes sin, don't partake of it." We are told to,

"Carefully determine what pleases the Lord. Take no part in the worthless deeds of evil and darkness; instead, expose them." (Ephesians 5:10-11)

As sons and daughters of the Kingdom, it is our responsibility to carefully determine what pleases God. If it is not clean by Biblical standards, don't partake of it. Let Philippians 4:8 be your guide, "Dear brothers and sisters, one final thing. Fix your thoughts on what is true, and honorable, and right, and pure, and lovely, and admirable. Think about things that are excellent and worthy of praise." These are the things we are to fix our thoughts on. Grieving the Holy Spirit and violating your conscience is not worth the fleeting entertainment.

Much wickedness comes through various forms of entertainment. Lucifer is in charge of the industry; he is the prince of the air. Consider this: all forms of sexuality, perverse joking, foul language, using God's name in vain, witchcraft, rebellion, revenge, and violence are in the average movie or T.V. show. Revenge and rage are central themes in some shows. Movies about the occult and witchcraft and books are prevalent in our culture. These forms of entertainment regularly incorporate a storyline of people sleeping together before marriage or living together, and homosexuality and sensuality are promoted more than ever.

The music industry is not any better. The mainstream music industry is steering the culture into utter corruption. Music is designed for worship and people don't realize the spiritual effects it has on the heart. It has the power to stir up carnal desires in you. Video games are a worldwide phenomenon. I read recently that the average gamer is in his 30's[4], and many games are violent with foul language. Think of what that constant corrupt input is doing to their hearts. This is what the world and many Christians inundate themselves with on a daily basis. Don't live by the world's standard.

"But now you must be holy in everything you do, just as God who chose you is holy. For the Scriptures say, 'You must be holy because I am holy.'" (1 Peter 1:15-16)

Notice this wasn't a suggestion but a command. "You must be holy". We can never handle sin or control the effects it has on our spirit. I can't drink poison and have it not affect me. Therefore, how much more should we guard our spirit over our physical body? Guard your heart beloved.

When we desire worldliness, we become worldly.
When we desire holiness, we become holy.

Have you noticed when you take part in carnal entertainment it affects your attitude? Remember what Peter said, "Dear friends, I warn you as "temporary residents and foreigners" to keep away from worldly desires that wage war against your very souls" (1 Peter 2:11). Peter uses strong verbiage in this text, "wage war" because Satan uses these ungodly desires to war, fight, and violently hurt your soul. Keep in mind, his motive is to kill and destroy (John 10:10). Two things begin to happen when we don't guard our hearts and protect our souls. We become completely numb and desensitized.

When you become desensitized by worldliness,
you are no longer sensitive to the Holy Spirit.

You will be fascinated by the world or you will be fascinated by God, but never by both. Demas was one of Paul's ministry workers and had served with him for almost five years. He had an honorable position serving Paul; however, he didn't endure and therefore was replaced. Look at what Paul told Timothy, "Be diligent to come to me quickly; for Demas has forsaken me, having loved this present world, and has departed for Thessalonica," (2 Timothy 4:9-10 NKJV).

Demas was serving one of the greatest ministry leaders of all time. Could you even imagine how incredible it would have been to serve Paul and the mission God had given him? As great of an opportunity as it was, Demas didn't guard his affections and the love of the world lured him right back in. Make this your prayer,

"Grant me purity of heart, so that I may honor you." (Psalm 86:11)

HOW TO DEAL WITH SIN

"You must warn each other every day, while it is still "today," so that none of you will be deceived by sin and hardened against God." (Hebrews 3:13)

Here's the good news, it doesn't have to take years to get free from sin! It can take place in a moment! First off, we must realize Jesus has already paid the price of our penalty of sin and through His death, He broke sins' power over us! Be encouraged and inspired by these verses of freedom,

- "When he died, he died once to break the power of sin." (Romans 6:10)
- "Sin is no longer your master." (Romans 6:14)
- "But now you are free from the power of sin and have become slaves of God. Now you do those things that lead to holiness and result in eternal life." (Romans 6:22)
- "And because you belong to him, the power of the life-giving Spirit has freed you from the power of sin that leads to death." (Romans 8:2)

It is scripturally clear that Jesus died to free you from the chains of sin. It is not His will for believers to be bound to sin. The reason many Christians are not walking in freedom is that many simply do not know the verses above nor claim the power of these verses in their lives. There are many Christians that just have the knowledge that Jesus died for our sins and paid the penalty. He did, but many don't know He also freed us from the power of sin itself. He freed us from that slavery. This is why renewing our mind is vitally important, knowing the truth and then acting on it is what sets us free. We just need to walk out that freedom.

Jesus taught us how to deal with strongholds or addictions while addressing the issue of lust. It doesn't surprise me that He used this sin. Lust is rampant in our society and one of today's main killers of marriages and destroyer of families. Recent statistics5 show that 79% of men and 34% of women between the ages of 18-30 view pornography in some form every month. When addressing lust, Jesus said, "And if your right hand causes you to sin, cut it off and throw it away. For it is better that you lose one of your members than that your whole body go into hell" (Matthew 5:30 ESV). This is Jesus' remedy for dealing with all sin of every manner, cut off anything that is causing you to sin.

What is causing you to sin? Is social media causing you to lust? Delete your account for a season until you are completely free. Is the internet on your phone or computer making it hard to resist looking at pornography? Get accountability software, such as Covenant Eyes and install it on all your electronic devices. Is a television show causing you to be greedy and covetous for wealth and riches? Cut that show out of your life. Are you listening to music that's arousing your flesh? Quit listening to that kind of music. Is your credit card causing you not to trust God? Cut up your card. Whatever is causing you to sin, cut it out of your life and "walk worthy of the calling with which you were called," (Ephesians 4:1 NKJV).

BECOME ACCOUNTABLE TO YOUR MINISTRY LEADER

There is power in accountability. No one is meant to do life alone and fight life's battles alone. We absolutely need each other. The enemy would love to isolate us and let us think we are supposed to fight the battles alone. Wolves love to isolate sheep. There is protection in the herd under the shepherd. Look at what James tells us:

"Are any of you sick? You should call for the elders of the church to come and pray over you, anointing you with oil in the name of the Lord. Such a prayer offered in faith will heal the sick, and the Lord will make you well. And if you have committed any sins, you will be forgiven. Confess your sins to each other and pray for each other so that you may be healed." (James 5:14-16)

There is power when you call on the leaders of the church to pray for you, there is forgiveness, healing and freedom. Don't let pride hold you back from being open and transparent with your ministry leader. God has placed that leader in your life to help you grow during this season, however your leader can only help you grow as much as you let them. What you bring to the light, loses its power it held while in the dark. It's time to remove impurities from your life, once these are removed you will be ready to serve the Master and your appointed leaders with excellence. It's time to become a Vessel of Honor, set apart as holy, useful to our Lord and Master, ready for every work God has laid out for your life.

Lord, I ask that you do a work of holiness in my heart. I want to live pure like Jesus lived. Purify and refine me. Expose any worldly passions and desires that are in my heart now. [Take a moment and allow the Holy Spirit to reveal impurities to you] I see the things that are displeasing to you, I nail these passions and desires to the cross now. Let me receive your grace to walk in purity and holiness. In Jesus' name, amen.

KINGDOM KEY #2
DEVELOP A
SERVANT'S HEART

Deep down inside, do you desire to be great? This isn't a trick question. There is nothing wrong with desiring to be great. The question is: why do you want to be great? Is it for your own glory or for God's? It's similar to money, there's nothing wrong with money – money is neither good nor bad. You can use it for good, or you can use it for sinful pleasures and to satisfy greed. It's the motive of what you want to accomplish with money that determines its productivity. The motive behind your desire for money directs it for God's glory or for sinful gain. Why do you want to be great? What is your core motive? Is it for you or Jesus?

The reality is God has called you to greatness! Let that sink in for a moment. You are His child. The heart of the Father is for you to be like Him. You were created in His image. Every godly father has a passion for their kids to accomplish greater things than themselves. If earthly fathers have that passion, how much more do you think our heavenly Father's heart longs for our success?

Whether or not you live out God's call on your life depends on whether or not you have a servant's heart. Jesus clarifies this when the mother of James and John asked Him to let her two sons sit on His right side and left side in the Kingdom. These seats were "places of honor". When the other disciples heard what James and John were requesting, they got angry and were indignant. Jesus saw the commotion and called them together to talk with them, it was then that He shared the greatest leadership principle. He made a stark distinction between worldly leadership and kingdom leadership. Jesus spoke first about leaders of this world who like to show off their authority and rule oppressively like tyrants. Yet this type of leadership should not be so among us,

> "If you want to be great, you must be the servant of all the others."
> (Matthew 20:26 CEV)

Notice Jesus didn't rebuke them or correct them for desiring to be great! Instead of rebuking them, He gave them the secret of greatness: Servants become Kingdom leaders who achieve greatness. Becoming a servant is the path to fulfilling God's great calling on your life. To fully understand what Jesus was saying you have to look at the Greek word He used for "great" the word is "megas", which means[1]:

1. persons, eminent for ability, virtue, authority, power
2. things esteemed highly for their importance: of great moment, of great weight
3. a thing to be highly esteemed for its excellence
4. splendid, prepared on a grand scale

Now with this understanding of the Greek word, what Jesus was saying in Matthew 20:26 was:

> If you want to be great (one that has power and authority, esteemed highly for your great moment of calling, and prepared for the grand scale) you must be the servant of all the others.

This may be hard to wrap your mind around, but this is what God sees in you, His child. Remember Jesus said, "He who believes in Me, the works that I do, he will do also; and greater works than these he will do; because I go to the Father" (John 14:12 NASB). Take ownership of the fact that God wants to use you to do great things in your life for His Kingdom. However, humility is the key to unlocking that greatness. Change your mindset and embrace the thought, "I must be the servant". I am challenging you to become the servant to everyone in your workplace, your family, and your church. Think of the team you currently serve on and make yourself the servant of all. Put yourself at the bottom and serve those around you!

Greatness is reserved for those who put themselves at the bottom, not for those trying to get to the top.

Who better to get leadership advice from then the greatest leader of all time? Not only did Jesus teach this, but He lived it. In Philippians 2 we see Jesus made Himself of no reputation, taking on the form of a servant, humbling Himself and God promoted Him. The title we should be passionate about is the title of Servant. This is the most beautiful and honorable title one could ever have. When we finish our race here on earth there is only one statement we all want to hear from God, "Well done, my good and faithful servant" (Matthew 25:23).

If Jesus humbled himself, you and I are going to have to humble ourselves. If you do not humble yourself, God will do it for you. Take action now to speed up the process and start receiving the rewards of humility. Humility always precedes honor (Proverbs 15:33).

The lower you go in humility,
the higher you go in the Kingdom.

CREATE A CULTURE OF HONOR

Now that you see the importance humility plays in the life of a believer and how essential it is, I hope you desire to grow in this area. To start our journey of growing in humility I want you to look at three translations of

Philippians 2:3 where Paul teaches us to,

- "Be humble, thinking of others as better than yourselves." (NLT)
- "In humility count others more significant than yourselves." (ESV)
- "With humility of mind regard one another as more important than yourselves." (NASB)

Paul is telling us to think of others as better, more significant, and important than ourselves. This was the mindset Jesus had and this is the mindset we should have too. Ask yourself, "Do I think of others as better than myself?" Is this an area you want to start growing in now?

Start praying for humility daily, make this one of your top requests and watch how God grows you. Most believers get caught up in praying for everything else in life and never ask for humility. It is common for people to pray for a new job, promotion, spouse, car, or home. These things are not bad; however, they can distract us from what is most important: becoming like Christ and winning the lost. I have found it is more beneficial to pray for humility than most other things.

As you begin to pray for humility daily, start looking for ways to honor your team members, co-workers, colleagues, and family members. Honoring others will automatically grow you in humility as honor requires a humbled heart. This is one area we are challenged to outdo one another,

"Love one another with brotherly affection. Outdo one another in showing honor." (Romans 12:10 ESV)

This is how you create a culture of honor! Lastly, I want to challenge you not to seek after titles or positions of authority. Those things will all come in the right season. In ministry, it is easy to lose focus of serving others and seek to serve yourself. The temptation often comes to desire a prominent title or position, but this is a trap to get our focus off of serving our leaders. This is a scheme of Satan to get us to focus on self-promotion and private ambitions. Our job is not to promote ourselves, that is God's job. We are told to, "Humble yourselves before the Lord, and he will lift you up in honor" (James 4:10).

Humility is the key to a servant's heart.

Lord, I see how important humility is and that you desire me to have a servant's heart. Help me grow in humility. Give me the grace to view others as more significant than myself. Help me to be the servant on my team, in my workplace, and within my home. In Jesus' name, amen.

KINGDOM KEY #3
BE LOYAL TO
YOUR LEADER

The reality is your calling, and future destiny is connected to your leader. The sooner people realize that, the sooner they are on their way to fulfilling their destiny. The Bible is full of examples of godly people serving their leaders. As their lives unfolded, their servanthood brought fulfillment of their own destiny.

- Joshua served Moses - Moses appointed his assistant Joshua to take his place as leader of the Israelites.
- Samuel served Eli - Samuel was trained in all ministry duties from Eli, which prepared him for his future role as one of the most influential prophets in the Old Testament.
- David served Saul - Throughout the years of serving he was developed as a leader as Saul promoted him through the ranks.
- Elisha served Elijah - As a result received his prophetic mantle of ministry.
- Timothy served Paul - Timothy was Paul's personal assistant. He was mentored by Paul and learned the ministry from him, preparing him to be the lead pastor in Ephesus.

Each of these were loyal assistants to their ministry leaders. As they served their leaders, they became equipped for their future ministries. Ruth served Naomi - Ruth recognized Naomi as a leader in her life, remaining loyal to her and as a result found her husband, family, and purpose. Look at the commitment level in Ruth's words to Naomi:

"Wherever you go, I will go; wherever you live, I will live. Your people will be my people, and your God will be my God. Wherever you die, I will die, and there I will be buried. May the Lord punish me severely if I allow anything but death to separate us!" (Ruth 1:16-17)

These were not empty words Ruth spoke, but rather a purposeful life lived in loyalty. Ruth served Naomi and followed her to Bethlehem, causing a release of favor over her life. When Ruth went to work in the fields, Boaz who was a wealthy and influential man ordered his staff to pull out grain from the bundles for her on the path she was working to bless her. It's interesting to note that her commitment and loyalty to Naomi were recognized by Boaz, who mentioned, "You are showing even more family loyalty now than you did before," (Ruth 3:10).

Keep in mind, "Loyalty makes a person attractive" (Proverbs 19:22). Loyalty, like honor, is a valuable trait that will cause you to stand out. Leaders are hard-pressed to find someone who is loyal to them, committed to them for the long haul— someone they can genuinely trust. This truly became a reality to me while I was traveling with my pastor on a ministry trip to Australia. An associate pastor from one of the churches we were visiting said to me, "Your role is amazing, not just because of what you do, but because he trusts you." What he said hit me like a ton of bricks. It was in that moment that I realized trust is rooted and built on the foundation of loyalty.

WHOSE SERVANT HAVE YOU BECOME?

Elisha was one of the greatest prophets of the Old Testament. He was Elijah's successor and received a double portion of Elijah's anointing, but it took seven years for that to become reality. While in waiting for his own ministry to begin, he walked alongside Elijah with remarkable faithfulness and loyalty.

When they first met, Elijah saw Elisha working in the field, approached him and threw his cloak on Elisha and walked away. That was a powerful and prophetic moment in Elisha's life because prophets were known to wear mantles symbolizing authority and calling. Elijah was giving him the opportunity to take part in his calling and ministry. Elisha's response is what determined the course of his life.

"Then he arose and followed Elijah, and became his servant."
(1 Kings 19:21 NKJV)

Elisha made a decision in that moment to commit his life to Elijah, he submitted himself to Elijah and became his servant. I need to ask you, whose servant have you become? Take a moment and recognize who God has placed in your life and become their loyal servant. Elisha stayed faithful to the end with Elijah, knowing that his destiny was connected to who he served. Had he quit serving Elijah one year earlier, he would have never received the anointing nor the prophetic ministry (2 Kings 2:10). It was imperative that he served him till the end.

DON'T MISS YOUR OPPORTUNITY TO SERVE

***Don't miss the opportunity you have right now
to serve your leaders and the vision God has given them
for your city.***

The story of the rich young ruler is perhaps one of the saddest stories in the Bible. This man had an opportunity to serve on the greatest ministry team of all time. The ruler runs up to Jesus, kneels before Him, and asks the question, "What must I do to inherit eternal life?"... Jesus, looking at him, loved him, and said, "You lack one thing: go, sell all that you have and give to the poor, and you will have treasure in heaven; and come, follow me" (Mark 10:17, 21 ESV). I love how it said Jesus loved him. Love will always tell you the truth. Love will always confront the area in your life that needs to be dealt with. Jesus will always find the one thing in your life, that one idol that is more important to you than Him. Jesus gave this man an invitation to join His team!

What happened after that? Did the young ruler go and sell all that he had? The Bible tells us he was, "Disheartened by the saying, he went away sorrowful, for he had great possessions" (Mark 10:22 ESV). He was not willing to make the sacrifice and commit to the ministry. This guy missed his opportunity of joining Jesus' ministry team and missed the opportunity to serve Jesus Himself. Imagine how his life might have been transformed, if he'd only been willing. Don't miss your opportunity to commit wholeheartedly and serve your ministry leader with a heart of loyalty.

During the seven years I spent serving my pastor, one of the main scriptures that encouraged me to remain consistent and loyal was 1 Samuel 3:1, "Meanwhile, the boy Samuel served the Lord by assisting Eli." Let this verse encourage and inspire you. When you serve your leader, you are in reality serving Jesus! Let that be your motivation for serving. Because of Samuel's servant's heart, he was raised up as the prophet in Israel. He anointed King Saul and David to be kings over Israel. He had a tremendous prophetic ministry and it all began with him serving Eli.

I want to challenge you this season to commit yourself to your pastor. Leaders need to know those on their team are with them and are in their corner. A great example of this is when Jonathan had a daring plan to attack the Philistines. Most people would have never attempted what he was planning, but look at the loyalty from his armor bearer:

"Do all that is in your heart. Do as you wish. Behold, I am with you heart and soul." (1 Samuel 14:7 ESV)

This depth of loyalty is Kingdom Honor. Does your leader know you are with them heart and soul to accomplish the vision God has given them? Oftentimes your leaders will have daring plans or vision that takes a tremendous amount of faith and commitment to pull off. Your leader needs to know everyone on their team is all in!

Lord, I recognize that my spiritual leaders need my loyalty. I see now that I can give them life and energy through my devotion to them. Help me to see them as the God-ordained leaders you created them to be. Help me to honor their place in my life through loyal service and dedication and help them fulfill the vision you have given them. In Jesus' name, amen.

KINGDOM KEY #4
RESPECT YOUR LEADER

"Dear brothers and sisters, honor those who are your leaders in the Lord's work. They work hard among you and give you spiritual guidance. Show them great respect and wholehearted love."
(1 Thessalonians 5:12-13)

In my opinion, one of the most dangerous sayings that has circulated the body of Christ is, "I don't want to put someone on a pedestal." Usually when people make that statement what they are meaning is, "I don't want to worship man." I wish they would just say that, because as Christians we are called to:

- Esteem others. (Romans 12:10)
- Think of others as more significant and important than ourselves. (Philippians 2:3)
- Have the mindset we are the servant. (Matthew 20:26)

There is a big difference between worship and honor. Worship and honor are summed up in the two greatest commandments, "'You must love the LORD your God with all your heart, all your soul, all your strength, and all your mind.' And, 'Love your neighbor as yourself'" (Luke 10:27). These commandments illustrate the difference between worshiping God and honoring people. God desires our love for Him to far supersede that of even our spouse and children (Luke 14:26). Worship is reserved for God alone; honor is directed toward God and man. Honor can also be found in the golden rule, "Do to others whatever you would like them to do to you" (Matthew 7:12). Can you see how damaging it can be to confuse the two? We now withhold honor from almost everyone in authority, not esteeming nor holding them in high regard.

We don't honor the president unless of course, it's someone we voted for. We can keep from honoring pastors unless their views reflect ours. We withhold honor from our coaches, teachers, or bosses unless it's someone we determine qualified. So, who really is the focus of our honor? Is it others or is it based on standards we have determined? Can that even be called real honor?

It is our calling to esteem everyone, elevate everyone, and hold everyone in high regard. I want to tell you to put people on pedestals! Put your wife, kids, brothers, sisters, and your leaders on pedestals. Remember, I am not talking about a pedestal on which to worship them. I am referring to a pedestal of honor that will remind you to "esteem others more highly than yourself".

"Appreciate those who diligently labor among you, and have charge over you in the Lord and give you instruction, and that you esteem them very highly," (1 Thessalonians 5:12-13 NASB)

VALUE YOUR LEADERS COUNSEL

Go to your ministry leader periodically and seek out their wisdom and counsel. Paul tells us, "They work hard among you and give you spiritual guidance" (1 Thessalonians 5:12). I remember when I first began working with my Pastor, I was so excited! I remember thinking, "He's going to pour so much wisdom, biblical revelation and knowledge into me. I'm going to learn so much about God, ministry, and leadership." I was surprised and a little disappointed during my first year when he didn't share nearly as much as I expected him to!

The Holy Spirit convicted me that I needed to pursue his counsel and wisdom. If there were things I wanted answers for or counsel, I was responsible for seeking him out. When I started asking questions, he started giving answers. When I started going to him for advice and counsel, he began to share with me. Years later, I can say I have learned so much from him, more than I even thought I was going to. Pastors and ministry leaders are not going to just share all their wisdom with you until you're ready to learn it, until you begin to pursue it, until you have a teachable spirit.

> *When you ask for their wisdom and counsel it shows them you value what they say, and respect them as a ministry leader.*

HOW TO MAINTAIN YOUR RESPECT FOR YOUR LEADER

Regarding our attitude towards church leaders, Paul instructs us, "Show them great respect," (1 Thessalonians 5:13). Another translation says to "esteem them very highly" (NASB), but how do we do this consistently? It's actually really simple: we respect the position and the authority God has given them, not their actions. Allow me to explain; not one of us is perfect, and that includes your pastor or leader. Not one of us lives our daily lives completely without sin. We all know this intellectually, but somehow, we incidentally believe they should be perfect, and we set an unrealistic expectation of them. With that mindset, you will be greatly disappointed when you realize they are in fact not perfect.

I don't say this to disrespect your leader in any way. However, it is important for us to realize our pastors or ministry leaders are not angelic beings. They are people who have given their lives to the call of God and are being refined day by day just like you and me. They are daily growing in their walks with God just as we are.

If you base your honor and respect on their actions, your attitude of honor will be like a roller coaster. One moment up and one moment down because one day they said, "Hi", and the next day they didn't. One day they said, "Thank you", and the next day they didn't. If your honor is based on their position rather than their actions, your level of respect will remain consistent. As mentioned earlier, one of the main descriptions of the word honor means: A valuing by which the price is fixed.[1]

This can be difficult because we have been trained by our culture to only respect someone if they earn our respect or if they respect us in return. Another selfish practice is to give respect to someone only if they make us feel good. That may be the culture of the United States of America, but that's not the culture of The Kingdom of Heaven. In the U.S., many respect political or spiritual leaders based on whether they like them or not. This is superficial respect based on actions but not based on the authority of their office. It's based on performance but not position. This means people have to perform to our expectations if they want our respect. Kingdom principle says, "I honor you because I recognize the authority you have, and the position you hold, even if I would do it differently than you."

Let me make this clear: You may not agree with everything they say or do, and that is okay. The key is to not allow your disagreement to lead you to become a vessel of dishonor. There have been times where I have not agreed with all the decisions my pastors or leaders have made. The most significant test you will go through is whether or not you will honor them even when you disagree.

We all have different ideas on how we would do things. The key is to always remain honorable! Too often when people don't get their way, they wear their emotions on their sleeves, walk around with a negative attitude, or worse vent their disagreement to others.

Keep this in mind: Don't honor your leaders because of what they do or don't do for you. Honor them because of what Jesus did for you! You and I didn't deserve anything Jesus did for us, right? Yet He honored us,

He esteemed us, He preferred us and gave His life for us when we did not deserve it. So likewise, we honor the office and the authority not because our leaders did anything for us, but because of what Jesus did for us.

Respect the God-ordained office, position, and authority your leaders have, and you will have unshakable honor.

THE FAMILIARITY TRAP

One of the traps people fall into when dealing with their leaders is familiarity. Familiarity can be the enemy of honor. What does it mean to be familiar? You fall into the familiarity trap when you think you are on your leader's level. When you begin to see/treat them as your friend rather than a God-ordained leader. Avoid becoming so familiar with your leader that they seem more like a friend than a God-ordained authority. This will protect you. I have seen people grow familiar with their leader and before they realize it, they have gone down the slippery slope into dishonor. I have talked with leaders, and this frustrates them greatly because in the beginning, their team members were on time, honorable, and respectful. Familiarity too frequently causes servants to become casual rather than honorable. Their spirit of excellence slips away.

Don't try to be their best friend.
Be their best servant!

Paul tells us to, "Outdo one another in showing honor" (Romans 12:10 ESV). Focus on honoring your leaders rather than being their buddy. There may be a friendship that develops between you and your leader, but allow your leader to open the door to developing it. If and when a friendship does develop, be ever vigilant to maintain a high level of respect and honor for them. Over the years serving in ministry together, my Pastor and

I have become friends. However, I always consider him Pastor first, friend second. If your relationship with your leader develops into friendship, always consider them leader first, friend second. This will keep you from falling into the familiarity trap and operating outside of honor.

I cringe when I hear people talk to their leader disrespectfully, calling them by a nickname or addressing them casually like, "Hey bro!" or using casual terms like "dude". Nicknames may be fine if you have been instructed to by your leaders, but if your leader is a pastor call them "Pastor". If they instruct you not to call them Pastor, ask them what they would like to be called. If your leader is not a pastor call them Mr./Mrs./Miss or Sir/Ma'am unless told otherwise. Defer to them, honor them with your addressment of them. This is one way to maintain a high level of respect. Remember when you were in grade school you called your teacher Mr. or Mrs.? It was a sign of respect because they were an authority figure.

Recently, when taking my car to get an oil change, the attendant said, "How's it going boss?" and "What can I do for you, boss?" I realized this was something they did to all their clients being served. This was a simple sign of respect and made me feel honored. We all like to be treated with respect.

When talking to your leaders, always respond with the utmost respect, "Yes sir" or "Yes ma'am". Sometimes in my mind, I remind myself God has appointed this leader as an authority in my life. I remind myself of the weight of their role, so I never take it lightly. This may shock you, but Paul tells Timothy to serve Christian leaders even better than unbelieving leaders.

"Bondservants regard their own masters as worthy of all honor, so that the name of God and the teaching may not be reviled. Those who have believing masters must not be disrespectful on the ground that they are brothers; rather they must serve all the better since those who benefit by their good service are believers and beloved." (1 Timothy 6:1-2 ESV)

DISRESPECTING YOUR LEADER WILL COST YOU

I was at a prayer meeting where a woman was asked by the pastor to stand on the platform and pray. When she was handed the mic, she began to pray passionately and with boldness, she stirred a hunger in everyone to pray. It was really evident she had a gift in her life and the grace to lead multitudes in prayer. The next day, I had caught her in passing and told her what an amazing job she had done, and I encouraged her to join the prayer ministry. I told her that she would become one of the leaders in no time. Her response shocked me as she hesitated for a moment and said, "I don't think I can serve under that pastor."

I was literally taken back and speechless. Here is a woman who has a tremendous gift that will lay dormant and not bear much fruit, all because she couldn't humble herself and serve under a particular pastor. What it really came down to was that she couldn't respect or honor the pastor. Do not let your lack of respect or lack of ability to honor your leader's God-given position and authority cripple you from fulfilling your calling.

Lord, I realize I am challenged to have deep respect for my leaders. I recognize you have established them in positions of leadership. I repent for not giving them the respect and honor as I should. Your Word says that I am to honor them, have deep respect and godly fear towards them. I desire this revelation to be true in my life. Help me to honor their position even when I don't agree. Help me to remember that I honor them not because they deserve it but because You honored me when I didn't deserve it. Holy Spirit, do a work in my heart to love and honor them as Your Word commands. I thank you for the pastors and leaders you have placed in my life and from this day on, I will commit to respect them in my heart, mind, with my words and actions. In Jesus' name, amen.

SECTION 2: SUMMARY

Key #1) Be a Vessel of Honor:
We must purify ourselves from sin and focus on becoming a vessel of honor. 'Therefore, if anyone cleanses himself from what is dishonorable, he will be a vessel for honorable use, set apart as holy, useful to the master of the house, ready for every good work" (2 Timothy 2:21 ESV).

Key #2) Develop a Servant's Heart:
Embrace the thought, "I must be the servant". Humility is key. Become the servant to everyone, at your workplace, in your family, and at your church. The lower you go in humility, the higher you rise in the Kingdom. "Do nothing from selfish ambition or conceit, but in humility count others more significant than yourselves" (Philippians 2:3 ESV).

Key #3) Be Loyal To Your Leader:
As Elisha was Loyal to Elijah, be Loyal to your ministry leader. Leaders are hard-pressed to find someone who is loyal, committed, and not going to jump ship — someone they can genuinely trust. As you loyally assist your leader, you are being trained and prepared for future ministry.

Key #4) Respect Your Leaders: Honor the God-ordained leadership, office, and authority. We honor the office and the authority not because our leaders did anything for us, but because of what Jesus did for us. We respect even if we don't agree with every action. "We ask you, brothers, to respect those who labor among you and are over you in the Lord and admonish you, and to esteem them very highly in love because of their work. Be at peace among yourselves" (1 Thessalonians 5:12-13 ESV).

SECTION 2: ACTION STEPS

1) Meet with your ministry leader or pastor and be open with them and transparent about any secret sin you are struggling with. We all have sins that can easily trip us up if we are not careful. Ask them to pray for you and to hold you accountable in this area.

2) Ask God to help you grow in humility. Ask Him to show you specific ways you can operate in humility towards those around you this week. "Love one another with brotherly affection. Outdo one another in showing honor." (Romans 12:10 ESV)

3) As Ruth was loyal to Naomi and Elisha left everything to serve Elijah, let your leader know this week that you are committed to them and you support them. Expressing your loyalty and dedication to Your Pastors and leaders is life-giving and energizing.

HOW TO HONOR YOUR LEADERS - PART 2

SECTION 3

KINGDOM KEY #5
OBEY YOUR LEADERS

Bear with me now, I know the word obey scares people sometimes. The word obey indicates submission to another, but the Bible says, "Obey your spiritual leaders" (Hebrews 13:17). We understand this in every other area of life. While growing up, we obeyed our parents, at work we obey our bosses, in our cities, we obey police officers, on sports teams we obey our coaches, and in school, we obey our teachers. We obey all these different types of authority figures and for some reason, the only place we don't think we have to obey is in our churches. Think about that for a moment. Isn't it surprising? In every other area of our life we obey, except the church. Yet the Word clearly tells us we are to obey our spiritual leaders because they are watching out for our souls. Look carefully at these scriptures:

"Obey your spiritual leaders, and do what they say. Their work is to watch over your souls, and they are accountable to God." (Hebrews 13:17)

"Remind them to be subject to rulers and authorities, to obey, to be ready for every good work." (Titus 3:1 NKJV)

"Slaves [servants], obey your earthly masters [leaders] with deep respect and fear. Serve them sincerely as you would serve Christ." (Ephesians 6:5)

"Slaves, obey your earthly masters in everything you do. Try to please them all the time, not just when they are watching you. Serve them sincerely because of your reverent fear of the Lord." (Colossians 3:22)

The word obey is in all of these verses, and each one refers to authority. You and I are to do what they ask; it is their job to disciple us and train us to do the works of the ministry (Ephesians 4:11-12). When you don't obey the spiritual leaders in your life, it is unprofitable for you. Look again at Hebrews 13:17:

"Obey those who rule over you, and be submissive, for they watch out for your souls, as those who must give account. Let them do so with joy and not with grief, for that would be unprofitable for you." (NKJV)

It is unprofitable for you and me when we disobey or dishonor those in leadership. Let that sink in for a moment. The good news is the opposite is also true, if we obey and listen to our spiritual leaders it will be profitable to us and we will succeed (2 Chronicles 20:20).

MY HARD LESSON

As a young man, I learned the hard way the importance of obeying my spiritual leaders. When I was 18 years old, God called me to join a ministry internship led by godly pastors and made it clear that he wanted me to remain in the internship for four years. After my third year, I began to pursue a relationship with a Christian girl from my church. Within the week, my pastor and his wife addressed me, sharing they felt that I should not be in this relationship. They were giving me the spiritual and practical wisdom I needed to hear. At the time, I couldn't believe they had even gotten involved. I thought they were 100% wrong. Who were they to tell me who I could and could not date? Ultimately, I didn't want them to tell me what I could or could not do. My pride blinded me, and I rebelled against their wisdom and counsel.

The reality was they were 100% right. Within a very short period, the relationship ended. I should have heeded the instruction of my pastors. I wish the story ended there, but it didn't: I decided not to do the fourth year of the internship. My rebellion and dishonor toward my leaders detoured me from the path God had originally told me to walk. To this day I remember a quote from my pastor, he said: "You lose nothing by waiting." This statement is so true. I would like to add to that, "You lose nothing by waiting, but you can lose everything by rushing."

Sometimes I wonder what might have been if I had obeyed God and completed the fourth year of internship. Looking back, I can see there were signs of dishonor that I wish I had recognized at the time. Each form of dishonor is rooted in rebellion in some form. I still loved God, read the Bible every day, prayed, and worshipped. This leads me to ask this question: Is the devil that crafty and that deceitful that he can get us to rebel against God and not even realize it? Isn't that essentially what deception is? In later chapters, we will discuss the signs and symptoms of rebellion, so you will be able to detect them early on and stop rebellion before it derails you.

EMBRACE CORRECTION

"If you ignore criticism, you will end in poverty and disgrace; if you accept correction, you will be honored." (Proverbs 13:18)

You and I need ministry leaders in our lives that we have given the freedom to correct us. We all have blind spots, and we need input from godly leaders around us to check our blind spots and help us correct them before we end up on the path of destruction. You need to be willing to humble yourself and give your leader permission to speak into your life with correction if they see you veering off course. Ask them to admonish you if they see you operating in pride, selfishness, or sin in any area of your life. It won't always be easy to hear, and it won't feel good, but it is essential to your growth that you seek out correction from them. When we do this, God works humility into our lives, ridding us of pride and dishonor, and prepares us to be honored by Him.

> "Likewise, you who are younger and of lesser rank, be subject to the elders (the ministers and spiritual guides of the church)—[giving them due respect and yielding to their counsel]. Clothe (apron) yourselves, all of you, with humility… that in due time He may exalt you." (1 Peter 5:5-6 AMPC)

Correction may be one of the hardest things to embrace. Our carnal nature fights against it every chance it can. We don't like change, and we don't like to be told we are wrong. I will never forget when I picked up my Pastor from the airport, and no sooner was he in the car than he began to correct me regarding a ministry I was overseeing. He was right, I needed the correction. He was not unkind, he gave the correction in a godly manner. But it was still hard on my flesh to hear. I did not show any outward signs of disrespect or disagreement, but inside, I was hurting.

I remember after he gave the correction, there was silence in the car for a few minutes, my pride stung, and I was feeling the embarrassment of correction keenly. The Holy Spirit spoke to my heart and said, "Are you going to be silent and offended the rest of this hour-long drive?" I knew I needed to humble myself and embrace the correction, so I quickly prayed and immediately felt the relief of humility. I asked my Pastor how his trip had gone, and we spent the rest of the drive in meaningful conversation.

Learning to love and welcome correction is a key component to those who desire to become a vessel of honor.

"To learn, you must love discipline; it is stupid to hate correction." (Proverbs 12:1)

I have looked at this verse in multiple translations and almost all of them said, *"stupid."* One other translation said, *"ignorant."* God could not be any clearer about the foolishness of those who hate correction. I don't know about you, but I don't want to be thought of as stupid by our Holy God. We need to make up our minds to love discipline and love correction.

"People who accept discipline are on the pathway to life, but those who ignore correction will go astray." (Proverbs 10:17)

Which path will you choose? The pathway to life or going astray? A life of honor or dishonor? A life of obedience and fulfillment or one of rebellion and despair? Will you accept discipline and correction or reject it? Here is the scary part, no one intentionally decides to go astray. It is a byproduct of disregarding correction. When you refuse correction, you will head down a detour road away from God's path for you. This is exactly what happened to the rebellious Israelites. God denied them their Promised Land and sent them back into the wilderness. This is why rebellion is so dangerous and needs to be exposed. You will forfeit God's promise in your life if you do not repent and eradicate what you are corrected in. Welcome correction from God and the ministry leaders He has placed in your life.

"Place yourselves under the authority of spiritual leaders." (1 Peter 5:5 GOD'S WORD)

WHEN DO YOU NOT OBEY?

This is a question that comes up often and is worth addressing. The purpose of this book is to teach you to honor your leaders and serve your local church with full commitment. That is my heart and passion. However, when going through the scriptures, there is clearly a time you do not obey a leader or pastor, and that is when they lead you to sin. It does not matter what position of authority they hold. You do not under any circumstance, submit to an authority figure asking you to sin, "If the godly give in to the wicked, it's like polluting a fountain or muddying a spring." (Proverbs 25:26) It does not matter what title or position they hold, let's take a look at some examples:

Regarding Secular Leaders:

- Instructed to Sin

Joseph is an example of staying the course when Potiphar's wife wanted to sleep with him. She used her position to continuously pressure him to have a sexual relationship with her. Joseph's response was, "How could I do such a wicked thing? It would be a great sin against God" (Genesis 39:9). He ran, and ultimately, it cost him his job and landed him in prison. If you ever lose anything because of obedience to God, rest assured that God has plans in motion to reward you far beyond what you can imagine. Joseph's obedience eventually led him to be promoted to second in command over all of Egypt.

- Commanded to Worship a False God

King Nebuchadnezzar commanded the entire nation to bow before the idol statue, and worship it when the music played. Shadrach, Meshach, and Abednego did not bow, even when, threatened to be thrown into the blazing furnace. Their response to the king was, "Your Majesty, that we will never serve your gods or worship the gold statue you have set up" (Daniel 3:18). Notice they still called the king "Your Majesty" when they addressed him. They were not rude or disrespectful to the office he held in any way, shape, or form. They honored his position, while being very clear they would never bow or worship the idol, even though it would cost them their lives. This speaks volumes of their character because many only obey God when they are promised blessings. Look how God rewarded them, "Then the king promoted Shadrach, Meshach, and Abednego to even higher positions in the province of Babylon." (Daniel 3:30)

They were promoted. Every time you do the honorable thing, God will honor you.

- Forbidden to Pray

A major test for Daniel arose when King Darius established a national law prohibiting prayer. Daniel could not and would not obey this law against prayer because it went against God's law. He still prayed three times a day. This obedience led him to be thrown into the lion's den. Just as we saw with Joseph, Shadrach, Meshach, and Abednego, sometimes your obedience to God will lead you into a very uncomfortable situation. Joseph put in prison, the three young Hebrew men thrown into the furnace, and Daniel sentenced to the lion's den. Daniel's honor for God, paved the way for the unimaginable. God sent an angel to shut the mouths of the lions, giving a miraculous sign to the king. Daniel's obedience had a profound impact on the nation, as the King declared Daniels God the living God who all should fear and Daniel prospered. (See Daniel 6:25-28)

- Ordered to stop Preaching and Gathering

Peter and John were commanded by the council members to stop preaching the gospel. They were even threatened by the leaders. Their response was, "Do you think God wants us to obey you rather than him? We cannot stop telling about everything we have seen and heard" (Acts 4:19-20). Our ultimate allegiance and obedience is to God. Unfortunately, what Peter and John went through is what we will see more of in these last days. We will see more laws established that violate God's law, and we will see persecution increase with the goal of shutting the Church down. We are instructed to not forsake the assembling of ourselves together. (See Hebrews 10:25)

Regarding Ministry Leaders:

It is sad to say, that in the last couple of years, there have been multiple prominent ministry leaders that have been exposed for having sexual relationships, mishandlings ministry finances or other immoral behavior. This is truly heartbreaking. Paul tells his young assistant Timothy, "You should know this, Timothy, that in the last days there will be very difficult times... They will act religious, but they will reject the power that could make them godly. Stay away from people like that! (2 Timothy 3:1, 5).

He also tells the Corinthian Church, "Now I have written to you not to keep company with anyone named a brother, who is sexually immoral, or covetous, or an idolater, or a reviler, or a drunkard, or an extortioner— not even to eat with such a person" (I Corinthians 5:11 NKJV). Paul is not talking about staying away from unbelievers, but rather those that call themselves Christians, who live in sin, make excuses, and justify it. The New Testament warns us that some who call them themselves Christians or ministry leaders will:

- · Attempt to bring us into bondage (Galatians 2:4)
- · Say God's grace allows us to live immoral lives (Jude 1:4)
- · Reject the power that could make them godly (2 Timothy 3:5)
- · Lure people back into sin (2 Peter 2:18)
- · Practice lawlessness themselves (Matthew 7:22-23)
- · Teach people to sin as well as commit sexual sin (Revelations 2:14-16, 20-23)

If you are under a ministry leader who is tempting you to sin or is asking you to sin, you are not to submit to that leader. Paul encountered this when false believers crept into the church and tried to bring them under bondage again. His response was, "we did not yield submission even for an hour, that the truth of the gospel might continue with you" (Galatians 2:5 NKJV). It is critical we follow Paul's example and never submit under such circumstances even for a moment. I realize there are many situations where a leader could cross the line and step into sin. If you are in a situation that you know is wrong or feel uneasy about, go to another pastor or ministry leader and get counsel on the matter.

I do believe many Christians are under godly church leaders, who have a heart to disciple and train people for the work of the ministry. Who live under this mandate: "Preach the word of God. Be prepared, whether the time is favorable or not. Patiently correct, rebuke, and encourage your people with good teaching" (2 Timothy 4:2). May we as believers welcome the correction and the rebukes from our leaders just as much as we welcome the encouragement. That we may become everything God has us to be!

Lord, obedience is difficult. So often I believe that my way is the right way. I want to obey my spiritual leaders even when my flesh wants to rebel. Help me to heed their instructions, ideas, and especially their correction Father. I want to be the wise man who accepts correction, not the fool who despises rebuke and loses his way. Soften my heart and teach me to love discipline, knowing that your Word declares, there will be a harvest of righteousness. In Jesus' name, amen!

KINGDOM KEY #6
SERVE YOUR LEADER LIKE
YOU WOULD SERVE JESUS

"Serve them sincerely as you would serve Christ... Work with enthusiasm, as though you were working for the Lord rather than for people." (Ephesians 6:5, 7)

Paul tells the Christians twice in this passage to serve their leaders as they would serve Jesus. This is how we are to serve those in positions of authority. The Bible does not say worship them like you would worship Jesus, however, it does say serve them like you serve Christ! (Ephesians 6:5, Colossians 3:22). Consider this, what if for the next three months Jesus came back to earth and He was your pastor or your ministry leader? How would you serve Him? When you have that answer, live it out by serving your leader that way. It will change your life!

If Jesus was your ministry leader for the next three months:

- Would you be late for your serving schedules?
- Would you be late to meetings?
- Would you be late to church?
- Would you miss church without reason?
- Would you serve half-heartedly?
- Would you slander a decision you didn't like?

WHAT TYPE OF SERVANT ARE YOU?

Before we dive further into the concept of serving as though you are serving Jesus Himself, let me ask you: What type of servant are you? There are two types of servants: One that is forced into slavery and one who chooses to be a slave. The one who is forced into slavery feels obligated to serve. The one choosing to be a slave made the choice to lay down their rights and become a slave. Paul the Apostle said, "I am a bondservant." This is someone who was free, then who laid down their life (all their dreams and their freedoms for someone else). I've been in ministry for twenty years now, and God has given me the privilege of seeing the different aspects of church and ministry that many are not privy to see. I have traveled to various churches around the world and have worked with multiple ministry teams. Let me put it plainly, I've seen the real servants and the hirelings. There is a vast difference between the two: The real servants have willingly and selflessly laid down their lives for others. The hirelings are those that are in ministry only for money, title or position (John 10:13). These individuals do not really care for others rather their own agenda fuels their drive.

I was once training a young man to serve in the area of hospitality, and he had the hardest time serving people. I had to continually address his lack of humility in servanthood. There was one incident where he became very angry. He began to complain about a woman he was volunteering with saying, "I can't stand the way she treats me, I'm not her servant." He was referring to a moment when she apparently walked by and flipped her hand, signaling for him to open the door. This set him off and made him feel as if he was being treated as her personal servant. I looked at him and said:

Everyone can act like a servant; the true test is can you still be a servant after you've been treated like one?

This was a principal I had learned years before from one of my pastors. It is not that I condone anyone being treated like a servant; however, it's moments like these when people are tested, and you see the heart of a person. This young man got the point and realized he had a lot of pride to deal with. Unfortunately, he didn't last but a few weeks more, he chose to walk away. Everybody can wear the mask, wear the servant's clothes, and say they are a servant. But true servanthood has very little to do with outward appearance and everything to do with having a true servant's heart. Think about it, if deep down in your core you view yourself as the servant, you will have no problem being treated like a servant. You will have the mentality, "I am the servant." You want me to wipe down the table? Sure. You want me to clean the parking lot? Sure. You want me to open the door for you? Sure. This is why Jesus had no problem washing his disciple's feet. He viewed himself as the servant of all servants.

Jesus was the ultimate bondservant. He laid down his freedom as God and came to Earth to serve and lay down his actual life for us. Jesus wasn't looking for monetary gain, titles, or positions. He had a servant's heart, set on doing his Father's bidding with excellence. He came to show us how to serve, and then made the ultimate servanthood choice in dying on the cross. We must use his example as our guide, and endeavor to serve our leaders as though we were serving Jesus Himself. The reality is, we are serving Jesus Himself.

HAVE A POSITIVE ATTITUDE

"Work with enthusiasm, as though you were working for the Lord." (Ephesians 6:7)

Paul tells us to serve our leaders as we would serve the Lord, and to do it with enthusiasm. This word enthusiasm[1] also means zeal, passion, and excitement. Practically applied, this means to serve with a positive attitude.

Developing this attitude starts with your words. This is especially important when applied to the words you speak when given a task or instruction. When your leader asks you to do something, start responding like this:

- Yes, Sir or Yes Ma'am!
- Absolutely!
- Will do!
- We'll make it happen!
- You got it!
- Consider it done!

Any of these responses are ideal especially when communicated with confidence and enthusiasm. Look at these responses from Biblical servants to their leaders:

- "Do what you think is best," the armor bearer replied. "I'm with you completely, whatever you decide." (1 Samuel 14:7)
- "Do all that is in your heart. Do as you wish. Behold, I am with you heart and soul." (1 Samuel 14:7 ESV)
- "Tell me what I can do to help you." (1 Samuel 20:4)
- "Let's go at once to take the land…We can certainly conquer it!" (Numbers 13:30)

These statements were life-giving and exhilarating to their leaders. This level of positivity and relentless drive to do the impossible for your leader will set you apart from the rest. The naysayers to Moses' vision were banned from ever entering the land they were promised, and they were struck dead with a plague. Their negativity cost them. On the other hand, God said: "But my servant Caleb has a different attitude than the others have" (Numbers 14:24). God granted Caleb and Joshua access to the promised land because of their honorable hearts and positive attitude of commitment to Moses' directives.

It revitalizes leaders when they have team members who will carry the load and serve faithfully with loyal hearts. Remember, whenever you serve your God appointed leaders you are serving God Himself. Don't you want to be the kind of follower that says, "Absolutely! We can make it happen!" If your leaders love that kind of response from you, how much more do you think it pleases the heart of the Father? Be known as someone who has a "Make it happen attitude."

TRY TO PLEASE YOUR LEADER ALL THE TIME

Yes, you read it correctly. This is what scripture says in regard to our leaders. " Try to please them all the time, not just when they are watching you. As slaves of Christ, do the will of God with all your heart" (Ephesians 6:6). It not only says it in Ephesians but also in two other books in the New Testament. This is how seriously Paul is emphasizing this principle of serving authority:

> "Slaves [servants], obey your earthly masters in everything you do. Try to please them all the time, not just when they are watching you. Serve them sincerely because of your reverent fear of the Lord." (Colossians 3:22)

> "Slaves [servants] must always obey their masters and do their best to please them." (Titus 2:9)

In three different books of the Bible, we are told to try to please our leaders. Other translations say similar things like to work with all your heart or to put your heart and soul into it. I remember reading this in Ephesians and thinking, this has got to be wrong or at least a stretch, surely this can't mean all the time. Come on, are we really to try to please them all the time? The Holy Spirit reminded me that in the secular workplace, many people are positive, kind, and obey their leaders when they are around. But when their boss is gone, they slander, gossip, display a negative attitude, slack off from their work, and do not have their leader's best interest in mind. This is not how sons and daughters of the Kingdom are to operate. We are to be honorable 24/7.

We should always aim to give our all, pleasing them when they are around or not. Remember, even if your leader does not hear the gossip or negativity being spoken about them, you are breeding a spirit of discord among the body and working directly against what the Holy Spirit wants to do in your church.

In 2 Samuel 23, the Philistine army had taken over Bethlehem and David and his men were in the cave of Adullam. While David was in the cave he made a simple comment to them, "Oh, how I would love some of that good water from the well by the gate in Bethlehem" (v15). He just made a comment, and didn't order anyone to get him water. He could have easily commanded it. Yet, all he did was make a comment, nothing more. Look at what three of his men did for him without David knowing:

> "So the Three broke through the Philistine lines, drew some water from the well by the gate in Bethlehem, and brought it back to David. But he refused to drink it. Instead, he poured it out as an offering to the LORD. 'The LORD forbid that I should drink this!' he exclaimed. 'This water is as precious as the blood of these men who risked their lives to bring it to me.' So David did not drink it. These are examples of the exploits of the Three." (2 Samuel 23:16-17 NLT)

David was so shocked that they went out of their way and risked their lives for him to get some water. He didn't even drink the water, but instead poured it out as an offering to God. Here's the implication: When you bless your leader to this degree, it will in turn bless the Lord. As extreme as this account of David's Mighty Men sounds, it revealed their heart to please and serve their leader well. I love the last part of the verse, "these are the examples of the exploits of the three" (v17).

What examples! Why would God even have this in scripture unless it was profitable for us today? Does this not line up with Ephesians, when it says to try to please them all the time? From this day on, decide you will be mighty men and women to your leaders, aiming to serve them as though they were Christ Himself, trying to please them all the time.

Lord, I confess it is not always easy to view serving my leaders as serving you Jesus. My own pride, selfishness, and sometimes laziness gets in the way. Let me always remember that you are the ultimate example as the perfect bondservant. You alone were willing to lay down your freedoms completely to ensure my free-dom from sin. Help me to be a willing bondservant every day. I want to honor my leaders through servanthood Lord because I know that by doing so, I am pleasing you. Remind me daily to view them as I view you. Remind me that my service to them is as important as if I was serving in the throne room of heaven. In Jesus' name, amen.

KINGDOM KEY #7
CULTIVATE AN
EXCELLENT SPIRIT

An excellent spirit is one of the most valuable traits you and I can have. People with an excellent spirit go the extra mile. They are not satisfied with average or subpar performance. They are passionate for excellence and always go above and beyond to ensure they achieve that status. "Whatever your hand finds to do, do it with *all your might*" (Ecclesiastes 9:10 NASB). This trait is what distinguishes you from the crowd. Every leader in the Bible went the extra mile. Jesus commanded, "If a soldier demands that you carry his gear for a mile, carry it two miles" (Matthew 5:41). Keep in mind, soldiers were authority figures, so Jesus was instructing us to go the extra mile for those in authority. Look at the profound impact an excellent spirit had on Daniel's life:

> "Then this Daniel distinguished himself above the governors and satraps, because an excellent spirit was in him; and the king gave thought to setting him over the whole realm." (Daniel 6:3 NKJV)

Notice the way Daniel distinguished himself above the rest, there was an excellent spirit in him. If Daniel can distinguish himself, you and I are also capable of distinguishing ourselves. You can decide to be average or excellent; the choice is entirely yours. The king had plans to promote Daniel because of his excellent spirit. Excellence and promotion go hand in hand. Excellence set Daniel apart from the crowd, causing him to be promoted, which gave him the place of influence God had purposed for his life. An excellent spirit will pave the way to promotion in your life and is played out in tangible ways within your workplaces and within your ministries.

"Do you see a man who excels in his work? He will stand
before kings; He will not stand before unknown men."
(Proverbs 22:29 NKJV)

ORGANIZATION RESULTS IN PRODUCTIVITY

When the queen of Sheba visited King Solomon, "She was overwhelmed. She was also amazed at the food on his tables, the organization of his officials and their splendid clothing, the cup-bearers, and the burnt offerings Solomon made at the Temple of the LORD" (1 Kings 10:5).

The queen was amazed at the organization of Solomon's officials. Organization is a trait of someone with an excellent spirit. Their car is clean; their house is clean; their office is organized. Their work projects are organized and in order. They are people of discipline and people who plan. People who plan are people who are successful. Successful people don't hope to be successful, nor wish to be successful, they expect to be successful. They set goals and hit the mark. These are not dreamers but doers. A lot of people dream of doing great things, but few make progress. Leaders are looking for their teams to score and win. If they give you a project, they want to have confidence it will be executed in a well-organized fashion. It may seem inconsequential, but organization is a valuable trait. Organization clears the path from clutter and puts you on the road to success.

Write down the dreams, visions, or projects that your leader wants to be accomplished and give them concrete dates that they will be accomplished by. At this point, it is no longer a dream but a goal. Break those projects down into smaller goals with due dates and deadlines to hit. A goal broken down into steps becomes a plan. Once there is a plan, it is time for action. Look how David was described;

> "Whatever Saul asked David to do, David did it successfully.
> So Saul made him a commander over the men of war."
> (1 Samuel 18:5)

I guarantee you David was an organized man. Success does not come without planning or by accident. David would not have been able to become the commander of the men of war without being organized. Those in leadership cannot afford to lack organization because then everything underneath them falls apart. Whatever you are asked to do, no matter how minor the task, do it successfully. If you serve with your heart and soul as David did, you will also be promoted just like David was promoted. Manage your time, make a plan, use the calendar on your phone or buy a physical planner and keep track of what you need to get done. Make it your aim and goal to please your leaders and those in authority. Go out of your way and go the extra mile. It always pays off.

BE ON TIME

People with an excellent spirit are on time. I cannot emphasize this enough. Always be on time. I had a volunteer who helped me serve our Pastor on Sunday mornings. I was responsible for getting his breakfast, setting the lounge, and having the PowerPoint message ready to review, as well as handling any communication with the media team. This young man wanted to help me, but he had a pattern of being late. One day I had to tell him,

"If you cannot be on time, you are not reliable."

I went on to explain that I would not feel comfortable taking the weekend off because I wouldn't be able to trust him to get the job done. He received what I said and made it his aim to be on time from that point on. He bought a loud alarm clock. He set the alarm clock and his phone alarm to make sure he never overslept again. He mastered this area in his life and we eventually hired him to work on staff with our team. He became a great manager, someone who was always on time and who has an excellent spirit. After four years, God promoted him and he started his own company. Make it your goal, to never be late or you might miss out on a future calling God has for you.

EXCELLENCE LEADS TO PROMOTION

When you are faithful in little tasks, you will be given much more. Some people wait for big assignments and don't value the little tasks, not realizing the significance behind them. Jesus shares a parable in Matthew 25 about three servants. The man in this parable is the boss or leader who was going on a long trip. This ultimately symbolizes Jesus and represents Him leaving earth until His return someday. He called together his servants and gave them each a portion of silver. These bags of silver represent your calling, job, assigned task; whatever has been entrusted to you. He gave five bags of silver to the first servant, two bags of silver to the second, and one bag of silver to the third. Each of these bags of silver/tasks was given to them "in proportion to their abilities" (v15).

The particular word used in this verse for abilities was the Greek word dýnamis meaning: Strength, ability, and power.[1]

It is a supernatural ability. The same Greek word is used in Acts 1:8 that says, "You will receive power [ability] when the Holy Spirit comes upon you. And you will be my witnesses, telling people about me everywhere". We all have different abilities and the word dynamis always refers to supernatural abilities. Look at what these servants did:

> "The servant who received the five bags of silver began to invest the money and earned five more. The servant with two bags of silver also went to work and earned two more. But the servant who received the one bag of silver dug a hole in the ground and hid the master's money. After a long time their master returned from his trip and called them to give an account of how they had used his money." (Matthew 25:16-19)

The master returned to evaluate what each of them did with the money (also known as your job, calling, or tasks). The first two servants multiplied what was entrusted to them. I want you to take note they did this apart from direct instruction from their boss. They did this all by themselves; the boss did not have to think of everything and give them every little detail and every idea. He entrusted his silver (talents, tasks, calling), and left it up to them whether or not they would grow it. Keep in mind, both servants knew their master, knew what his interests were, and what he wanted to accomplish.

> "Workers who protect their employer's interests will be rewarded." (Proverbs 27:18)

There have been several projects that I have worked on for my Pastor that I just knew he wanted to do. I would always do what was asked of me, but then I would always ask God, "What else can I do? How can I use the ability you gave me to multiply this ministry?" This type of ability ownership brings great rewards in your life. Your leader doesn't want you to be a worker; they want you to be a leader, taking the initiative, improving projects, dreaming, and making things better. Look at the boss's response to the two servants who invested and increased what was given to them:

"The master was full of praise. 'Well done, my good and faithful servant. You have been faithful in handling this small amount, so now I will give you many more responsibilities. Let's celebrate together!'" (Matthew 25:21, 23)

Both servants had been faithful in handling this small amount. They both were rewarded with many more responsibilities. Responsibilities represent an increase of authority, a promotion. Both servants doubled what was given to them, and both received even more authority. Unfortunately, this was not the case with the last servant:

"Then the servant with the one bag of silver came and said, 'Master, I knew you were a harsh man, harvesting crops you didn't plant and gathering crops you didn't cultivate. I was afraid I would lose your money, so I hid it in the earth. Look, here is your money back.'" (Matthew 25:24-25)

It is evident this last servant had a spirit of fear in his life that held him back from accomplishing more. He was insecure in his ability. We can all learn from this example. How many people miss their callings because of fear or insecurity? He was paralyzed by fear and it kept him from multiplying; all he did was maintain what was given to him:

"But the master replied, 'You wicked and lazy servant! If you knew I harvested crops I didn't plant and gathered crops I didn't cultivate, why didn't you deposit my money in the bank? At least I could have gotten some interest on it.' Then he ordered, 'Take the money from this servant, and give it to the one with the ten bags of silver. To those who use well what they are given, even more will be given, and they will have an abundance. But from those who do nothing, even what little they have will be taken away. Now throw this useless servant into outer darkness, where there will be

Jesus called this servant "wicked and lazy". The servant could have done something, anything to increase what was given and did not. He didn't go to anyone for help. He could have at least put the money in the bank, and it would have increased through interest. He could have gone to those that were doing well and asked for advice and counsel. "Where there is no counsel, the people fall; But in the multitude of counselors there is safety" (Proverbs 11:14 NKJV).

Just like the master in the parable, your ministry leader is going to entrust you with tasks that you have the ability to do. As a ministry leader of several departments, it was my job to put people in the right position where they could thrive. Those that had a gift of hospitality, I placed them in the service of our pastors, hosting our guest speakers, or in customer service. Those that had creative abilities I would entrust creative projects, such as video editing, graphic design or stage building. Those that had business ability, I would place them in areas of management like the bookstore, café, or social media marketing and communications. I entrusted each person with the tasks I knew they had the giftedness to accomplish. As their leader, I expected them to not only accomplish those tasks, but cultivate an excellence of spirit that would lead to multiplication within the ministry.

Just remember not to be like the lazy servant. How can you take the small task that has been given to you and make it better; how can you take it to another level? If you are in a place where you don't know what to do to help your ministry department grow, seek counsel from those who have done well in your field. You have to seek wisdom and learn from those who have done more than you. Read a book, watch a course, go to a conference, travel to meet with a ministry leader - invest in yourself! When you invest in the talents and callings given to you by God, you honor Him and His Kingdom. You are acting as a good steward and this pleases God's heart. Whatever you do, don't just maintain what your leader gave you. Increase it!

"Work hard and become a leader." (Proverbs 12:24)

An excellent spirit goes the extra mile and excels in all areas they are entrusted.

Lord, it is so easy to do the bare minimum in life. I now realize serving my leaders; is really serving you. Every completion of every task should be made with the knowledge that I'm completing it FOR YOU. I want to take the gifts you've given me and multiply them for Your Kingdom. I want to be exceptional for you Jesus because you deserve my very best. The leaders you've placed in my life deserve my all. Help me cultivate an excellent spirit in all areas Lord. Not for my own glory, but yours. In Jesus' name, amen.

KINGDOM KEY #8
BUILD YOUR
LEADER'S VISION

Everything in the kingdom is the opposite of the world. If you want to be great, become the least. If you want to lead, then serve. The first will be last, and the last will be first. If your enemy curses you, bless him. If you want to be blessed, be generous and give. These principles are totally opposite to what we are told in the world. The world says, "Don't build another person's vision, build your own."

**If you build another man's vision,
God will build yours.**

Do you have a dream from God? That dream is a glimpse of your future ministry. Take that dream and put it on the shelf for now. Serve another's vision, build another's dream. This makes no sense to the carnal mind, but this is kingdom thinking: Putting others first. I hope this resonates with you because sometimes we get caught up in our own dreams and our own visions and we miss what God really wants to do in and through us. Jesus said,

> "And if you have not been faithful in what is another man's, who will give you what is your own?" (Luke 16:12 NKJV)

Before God gives us our ministries or fulfills the dreams He has given us, we must first fulfill the task of being faithful with our leader's vision. When we do this, we learn from experience about how dreams are fulfilled, and vision is accomplished. Remember, Elisha served the prophet Elijah for seven years before getting his mantle and prophetic ministry. Timothy served the apostle Paul and traveled with him for several years before becoming the lead Pastor of Ephesus.

SERVING IS BUILDING

What does it mean to serve? Does it mean to get your leader water when they are thirsty? Yes. Does it mean to get them coffee when needed? Yes. Does it mean to show up early to the ministry events? Yes. Does it mean opening a door? Yes. Setting up chairs and volunteering in different areas? Yes. Does it mean praying for them in times of need? Yes. These are all parts of honorable serving. However,

The greatest level of serving is when your leader's dream becomes your dream.

When this takes place, you are no longer just a worker, but a builder and even more so a leader. You're not just someone who adds to the ministry, you are a multiplier. You're not working for your leader; you're working with your leader. There is ownership that takes place. This isn't just your leader's ministry; it's your ministry.

God has given your leader dreams, but let me tell you this, God has not given them the full picture or all the details. Your leader may have a dream to do a worship album, have a T.V. show, or a men's ministry that makes a global impact. Your leader likely did not have all the details filled in for them by God when He gave them the vision. This is where servant leaders like yourselves come in. Leaders who serve alongside their pastor will be the driving force behind the details of the dream coming to fruition. Each leader has a dream, and everyone on the team has a significant part to play. Everyone has a supernatural gift from God that is useful for building the Kingdom. Remember, there is a reason God does not give the whole picture to just one person. Everyone is a part of the dream and vision becoming a reality.

When you fulfill your leader's dreams, your dreams will come to pass because they are connected.

Allow me to illustrate this to you through the life of Joseph. God gave Joseph two dreams of his future when he was just a teenager. They were not very detailed, a bundle of grain and a group of stars, but both alluded to Joseph one day ruling over his family. Shortly after receiving these dreams, Joseph was sold into slavery by his own brothers. Slavery. The opposite of ruling. He served Potiphar well, became head of the household, and maintained his righteousness through the debacle with Potiphar's wife. The wrongful accusation landed Joseph in jail, but even there he became a faithful servant to the warden, becoming a leader within the prison. Sold into slavery, wrongfully accused, thrown into jail, and yet, God had Joseph right where He wanted him.

Pharaoh's cup-bearer and baker were later imprisoned in the same jail, plagued with strange dreams. Whom better for them to meet then Joseph, king of dreams? Joseph interpreted their dreams and in three days, his interpretations came true. This moment was so pivotal in Joseph's life because one day two years later, Pharaoh had a dream that no one, not even his magicians and wise men could interpret (Genesis 41:8). It was then the chief cupbearer remembered Joseph, the man who interpreted his dream two years earlier. He quickly spoke up telling Pharaoh about Joseph and his ability to interpret dreams. Pharaoh sent for Joseph right away and Joseph was able to interpret Pharaoh's dreams. The Lord placed Joseph in that exact position at that exact time to warn Pharaoh of the upcoming famine that would decimate his land.

Here is where we are shown the difference between a worker and a leader. Joseph could have just interpreted the dream and done what was asked, but because he had a servant's heart, he went a step further and provided the solution that would save all of Egypt. Pharaoh was so impressed he asked his officials,

> "Can we find anyone else like this man so obviously filled with the spirit of God?" (Genesis 41:38)

When you are filled with the Spirit, your leaders will recognize it through your wisdom and ideas. Joseph's ideas and suggestions were what set him apart. The rest of Joseph's story is history. The burden of captivity was lifted from him and he was immediately put in charge over the entire land and led the people into great wealth and prosperity. He honored the Lord by serving Pharaoh and was rewarded 1000 times over. Three things stand out to me about Joseph and the kind of man he was:

1. No matter what situation Joseph found himself in, he honored every authority in his life.
2. He embraced his leaders' actual dreams as his own.
3. He brought his leader's dreams to fruition with practical solutions with guidance from God.

When you compare Joseph's and Pharaoh's dreams, they were one and the same. God showed Pharaoh one part of the vision and Joseph a different part of the vision. This is why unity is so important. Only through the fulfillment of Pharaoh's dreams could Joseph's dreams come true. Through Pharaoh's dreams, Joseph became ruler over all of Egypt, just as his own dreams foretold. What solutions do you have to advance the ministry you serve in? As you take on their dreams as your own and help them come to fruition, God will fulfill your dreams too.

Pharaoh had the dream, and Joseph had the solution.
Your leader has the dream, and you have the solution.

Every servant leader brings solutions to the table. Both Joseph and Daniel brought solutions to the table and solved problems. This is a trait that will set you apart. Most people bring problems and issues to the table, but leaders always recognize those that deliver solutions.

As I am writing this book, our world is in the middle of a global crisis with the COVID-19 virus. Large portions of the world remain shut down and everything has gone online in an effort to slow the spread of the virus. Churches are meeting largely online and through social media live streams. Small groups and ministry leaders are gathering via live video meetings. We are in uncharted ministry waters. As our Pastor has been learning how to become a virtual shepherd, he has relied heavily on his ministry team to come up with creative solutions to continue Kingdom work during crisis. This is only the beginning. God is not surprised by this crisis.

"There will be great earthquakes, and in various places plagues and famines; and there will be terrors and great signs from heaven." (Luke 21:11 NASB)

Events like COVID-19, intense earthquakes, fires and plagues are only going to become more frequent. Our ministry leaders need us to act as servant leaders. Take initiative, provide solutions and creative ideas to continue to advance the Kingdom. They need us to remain in the Word, and in His Presence, ready to stand alongside them on the frontlines of ministry.

DO YOU KNOW YOUR LEADER'S DREAMS?

What are your pastor's or your leader's dreams? What are some projects he or she has always wanted to accomplish? If you don't know, go to them and ask. God has placed you in their life to help them fulfill those dreams in this specific season. They cannot do it on their own, they need your help to achieve them.

Furthermore, pray and ask God for creative ideas that are in alignment with your leader's dreams and vision. There are some things I have accomplished for my Pastor that he didn't ask me to do, I just knew what aligned with his vision and what would achieve his goals. For example, He was preparing to preach an upcoming six-part series on evangelism. I was inspired to create short films that he could use during his messages to help drive home key points. I gathered my media team together two months before the series started and we began brainstorming. We created three films, one on the importance of evangelism, another about how not to evangelize, and the third exposed Satan's agenda. Pastor and the church loved these videos.

Another example of knowing my leader's dreams came when Pastor was doing child dedications. During the ceremony, he became emboldened to speak about the racial divide in our nation. I knew that was a powerful moment and needed to be on social media. I quickly posted the video, and it went viral, gaining over 50,000,000 views between several different social media outlets. This significantly boosted his social media presence and we have continued posting clips to spread the gospel on social media. I knew he wanted to find a way to reach out beyond our community, so I found a solution and God blessed my efforts.

I spent a lot of time traveling with my Pastor and he was often asked to teach on leadership principles. I sat in many of these training meetings and noticed how his material changed the lives of those who were in attendance. The principles he shared impacted every group he spoke to. I asked him if we could film leadership videos to spread these life-changing biblical leadership principles with a wider audience. We ended up developing the videos into a leadership course and even a book.

I sat with a fellow pastor's assistant and asked him if he thought his pastor had a book in him? Or did he have a preaching series that can be turned into a book? He said, "Oh yes, definitely!" I told him to help him write it. I also asked him, "When your pastor travels, does he bring materials and resources?" He said no, so I told him to get his pastor's sermons and package them so that when he travels, he can offer them as a resource to churches. This will help spread the Gospel further and bless the ministry. If your leader preaches and teaches, consider how you can get their resources to as many people as possible. Honor them by helping them accomplish their vision. You are honoring God in the process!

I challenge you to ask God for wisdom, solutions, and creative ideas for your ministry to advance the Kingdom. The Bible tells us if you lack wisdom ask God, He'll give it to you generously! (James 1:5)

> **When you serve the vision God has given your leaders, your gifting and calling will be revealed, developed, and fulfilled.**

Lord, My flesh wants to pursue the dreams you've given to me first. I don't always want to build my leader's vision, I want to build mine. Lord help me to remember that my dreams are connected to my leader's. Help me to see clearly that through building their dreams, I am being trained to be more effective in the eventual fulfillment of my own dreams. Help me to remember that you Lord, gave my leader their dreams and that by helping them build, I am building YOUR vision. In Jesus' name, amen.

SECTION 3: SUMMARY

Key #5) Obey Your Leaders: We all have blind spots, and we need input from godly leaders around us to check our blind spots and help us correct them before we end up on the path of destruction. "Obey your spiritual leaders and do what they say. Their work is to watch over your souls, and they are accountable to God" (Hebrews 13:17).

Key #6) Serve Your Leader Like You Would Serve Jesus: When we serve in ministry, we are ultimately serving Jesus and God Himself! Serve with a bondservant heart and positive attitude, be the Make-It-Happen team member. Try to please your leader all the time, this pleases the heart of your Father. "Slaves [servants], obey your earthly masters in everything you do. Try to please them all the time, not just when they are watching you. Serve them sincerely because of your reverent fear of the Lord" (Colossians 3:22).

Key #7) Cultivate an Excellent Spirit: An excellent spirit goes the extra mile and excels in all areas they are entrusted. Be organized, on-time, and plan to be successful. Those who are excellent with the small will be trusted with the great. "Whatever you do, do it with all your might" (Ecclesiastes 9:10 NASB).

Key #8) Build Your Leader's Vision: Before God fulfills our dreams He has given us, we must first fulfill the task of being faithful with our leader's vision. When we do this, we learn from experience on how dreams are fulfilled, and vision is accomplished. "And if you have not been faithful in what is another man's, who will give you what is your own?" (Luke 16:12 NKJV). Keep in mind,

When you serve the vision God has given your leaders, your gifting and calling will be revealed, developed,and fulfilled.

SECTION 3: ACTION STEPS

1) Go to your ministry leader and give them the authority to correct anything off in your life. Any pride, selfishness, bad attitude, or any area that is veering you off course or hindering you.

2) Is there an area of the ministry you are involved in that you don't particularly enjoy? Meditate on this verse, memorize it, repeat it to yourself anytime you are struggling with positivity in this ministry area. Resolve to work with a positive attitude.

"Work with enthusiasm, as though you were working for the Lord." (Ephesians 6:7)

3) What are some of the tasks, large or small that you are responsible for within your ministry? How can you go the extra mile with some of these tasks, can you be more efficient?

Remember: Excellence with the small tasks leads to entrusting with greater. (Matthew 25:21, 23)

4) Ask God for wisdom, solutions, and creative ideas for this ministry. (James 1:5) As a ministry leader myself, I can't tell you how encouraging it was to get emails, or text of new ideas. It shows me my team cares about the ministry and they are dreaming.

SECTION 4

HOW TO HONOR YOUR LEADERS - PART 3

KINGDOM KEY #9
GIVE DOUBLE
HONOR

"Let the elders who rule well be counted worthy of double honor, especially those who labor in the word and doctrine. For scripture says, "You shall not muzzle an ox while it treads out the grain," and, "The laborer is worthy of his wages." (1 Timothy 5:17-18 NKJV)

The only place in the Bible we see the term double honor is when used to describe how we are to take care of our ministry leaders. What specifically is double honor? We are called to honor our president, law enforcement officers, bosses, the CEO of our company, our spouse, etc. But this verse says we are to give double honor to those who labor in the Word. Look at the New Living Translation: "Elders who do their work well should be respected and paid well, especially those who work hard at both preaching and teaching" (1 Timothy 5:17).

Double Honor = Paid Well

Paying double honor equals giving financial appreciation and support for the work these leaders do in the ministry. It is expressing monetarily how much you value them. Does your ministry leader rule well? Are they edifying and equipping you for ministry? Then this verse says they deserve double honor. The verse goes on to say the laborer is worthy of his wages. A major problem we have right now is most churches are not taking care of their pastors. A poll states 57% of pastors can't pay their bills.[1] This is staggering but explains why many churches are struggling. If 1 out of every 2 pastors are experiencing financial hardship, this can lead to depression and stress in ministry, or eventually getting burnt out. While in the service of my Pastor, I saw fully the attacks senior pastors go through. I have served under managers in the secular field and managers in the church. As a result, I am convinced pastors have the hardest job and calling in the world. Not only do they have to ensure the bills get paid and the daily operations of the church run smoothly, but they are also watching out for the souls of their congregation and fighting daily spiritual warfare. The enemy is fully aware of the influence your ministry leader has and the potential your church holds to change a city. If there is one person Satan would love to take out or cause to throw in the towel, it's your leader. Your leader needs to know they are loved and supported. The devil is continually trying to tear them down with thoughts like:

- You are not making a difference in your city
- No one got anything out of your sermon
- Are you sure you should be pastoring?
- If you preach that message, people will leave your church

On top of this, their financial pressures are weighing them down. Recent statistics say 63% of pastor's wives feel finances are a prime source of stress for their family[2]. I really want you to think about this, 6 out of 10 ministry leaders have financial stress. This wears on their family and their marriage. Many of them can't even cover their bills. Financial stress is a leading cause of divorce[3]. I want to challenge you to practice this principle of Double Honor. Every two or three months, find some way, somehow to bless your leader. Get them a card or note that says thank you, give them a gift card, cash or check. Offer something letting them know you greatly appreciate them. Do what you can. Tell them it is an honor to serve on their team and what they mean to you. Show your leaders double honor and watch what God does for you. Remember, it is not the size of the gift.

We all make different amounts of income, but what matters is that we all show appreciation the best way we can. God looks at the heart not the wallet. Remember, it was the widow that gave two coins that moved the heart of Jesus (Mark 12).

Appreciation never gets old!

From my experience as a ministry leader, I can honestly say that when my team members express appreciation, it is a huge blessing to my family. We have been shocked and greatly encouraged that we are making a difference to those we lead. Recently, the team called my wife and I into the office to present a gift basket with all kinds of gift cards, some to restaurants, some to clothing stores, as well as gifts for our daughter. We were blown away and my wife was moved to tears!

This kingdom principle of giving gifts to your leaders is found throughout the Old and New Testament. When Saul and his servant were seeking direction from the prophet, they insisted on bringing him a gift! They didn't have much to offer, but they wanted to give him something and they had one small piece of silver. (see 1 Samuel 9:6-8)

"Those who are taught the word of God should provide for their teachers, sharing all good things with them." (Galatians 6:6)

"If we have sown spiritual things among you, is it too much if we reap material things from you?" (1 Corinthians 9:11 ESV)

Don't ever feel your gift is too small or insignificant. In the first book of Samuel, we see Saul and his servant still offered one small piece of silver. It's not the amount that matters, but your heart. Look at what Paul said when taking an offering: "I don't say this because I want a gift from you. Rather, I want you to receive a reward for your kindness." (Philippians 4:17). There is a reward that goes to believers who partake in double honor and it can be physical or spiritual. The main point is that through your obedience to the Lord, the Lord will reward you in a multitude of ways. Paul went on and bragged on them and thanked them for providing for him financially. He even went as far as to say that no other church did this for him. In fact, he declared over them: "And this same God who takes care of me will supply all your needs from his glorious riches," (Philippians 4:19).

Here are some ways we have given our Pastor and his wife double honor, hopefully, these will spark some ideas in you of how to bless your own leaders:

- Noise canceling headphones. We knew these would bless him considering how much he travels. My whole team pitched in on this gift and presented it to him. For months after, he told me how much they blessed him.
- Tickets for a football game, we know how much he enjoys sports.
- New walking shoes, as he enjoys exercise.
- A gift card to allow our Pastor's wife the ability to attend an out of town conference.
- Worship albums for our Pastor's wife, knowing how much she loves music.
- Sending him and his wife on a vacation.

Think about what your leaders love to do. Be creative! There are all kinds of things you can do to bless your leaders. You may want to make a meal for them or surprise them with their favorite dessert. You could offer to help clean their car, house or watch their children for an evening, so they can have a date night.

Consistent gifts with notes of appreciation will encourage them more than you will ever know. Also, it is an opportunity for your leaders to get a glimpse into your heart for them. You must be intentional about honor and plan it out. Make it a habit to honor your leaders throughout the year. Here are five recurring events each year to help you get started with being consistent: Birthdays, Pastor Appreciation, Thanksgiving, Christmas, and wedding anniversaries.

"A man's gift makes room for him; And brings him before great men." (Proverbs 18:16 NKJV)

When you present your leaders gifts out of a heart of honor, it will make room for you and open doors that only God can open. When someone values, honors, and respects those in authority, they are ready for promotion.

Lord Jesus, I understand how important it is for me to encourage my leader in practical tangible ways. Help me to do so on a consistent basis, with love and honor in my heart. Keep me from resenting this important responsibility by reminding me that my leaders are worthy of being paid well for they are watching over my soul. Help me not to be caught up in how extravagant the gifts need to be but remember that my leader will be honored by whatever I give, as long as my heart is right before you. In Jesus' name, amen.

KINGDOM KEY #10
GUARD YOUR
LEADERS

In the last two years, three ministry leaders in California took their own lives. These ministry leaders were suffering from depression and it overwhelmed them. One of these leaders was a mentor of mine. He had been serving in ministry for decades and his ministry helped lead thousands of teenagers to Christ. When I received the news of his passing, I was devastated. My heart was broken as I realized just how important support ministry is in the lives of our leaders. If you are an armor-bearer, assistant, secretary, volunteer, or intern, you play a very vital role in your ministry team.

During these last days, the ministry is getting harder, and our leaders are fighting attacks from all directions. Many churches are closing their doors and ministry leaders are leaving the ministry due to these dark days. Current Barna President predicts that 20% of churches will close down within the next 18 months.[1] Here are some additional statistics for ministry leaders over the last few years[2]:

- 54% of ministry leaders are overworked
- 43% are overstressed
- 34% battle discouragement
- 26% are overly fatigued

Our church leaders are under attack, and they need us to guard them. I can see the positive impact having served my Pastor with honor has had on him and his ministry through the years. Having been a ministry leader myself, I can attest to the fact that every leader needs an Elisha. Every leader needs people who come alongside them to help carry out the vision God has for their ministry. You and I can make a significant impact on our city and church by serving the leaders God has placed in our lives and guarding them from the attacks of the enemy.

"He who guards his master will be honored."
(Proverbs 27:18 ESV)

This verse says the one who guards his master will be honored. However, the opposite is also true, he who does not guard his master will not be honored, elevated nor promoted. When you guard your leader, you sincerely value them and are looking out for their best interest, not yours.

The Hebrew word used in this verse for the word "guards" is shamar[3]:

- to hedge about (as with thorns)
- guard
- protect
- attend to

GUARD AGAINST SPIRITUAL ATTACKS

You might rarely find yourself in a time when you have to protect your leader physically, as seen in David's relationship and guarding of King Saul. David had opportunities where he could have killed or allowed Saul to be killed to expedite his route to the throne. Time and again we see how David chose to protect Saul in vulnerable times. Most of the time the attacks you will be up against are spiritual.

"Then Saul would become refreshed and well, and the distressing spirit would depart from him." (1 Samuel 16:23 NKJV)

There are many types of spiritual attacks. Some are distressing spirits, others are verbal attacks, such as criticism, slander, accusation, or gossip. There will be many times you will be able to head off the attack yourself. There have been many attacks sent to distress my Pastor that I was able to dissolve without involving him. There have been times when attacks come through social media and I would take care of the issues and never bring them to his attention.

On the other hand, there have been times where I have had to involve my Pastor in the attack. One incident occurred when a leader was openly opposing a foundational doctrine that our Senior Pastor and his wife taught. This person verbally expressed his disagreement with two of my team members. Shortly after, he did the same thing in a staff meeting when the pastor was not present. I struggled with this for a few days. How do I address it? I mean, who would want to bring something like this up? Yet, I saw how destructive a spirit of division could be among teams. There is nothing wrong with having different views of doctrine. There is something wrong when you share or teach your contrary opinions to others in your church without your pastor knowing it.

After four long nights, the Holy Spirit impressed on my heart that I needed to tell my Pastor and his wife. He was grateful I had. The leader was swiftly confronted, humbled himself and quickly came to repentance. There was reconciliation, and since then God has promoted him in his ministry and has done amazing things through him. Be prepared, oftentimes when guarding your leader, you'll absorb the spiritual attacks. This is why it's crucial you are spiritually fit, honoring the Word daily. Not only are you battling your hardships, but you are standing against attacks that come toward your leader.

GUARD AGAINST BURNOUT

Today 26% of ministry leaders are overly fatigued and 54% are over-worked[4]. While 91% have experienced some form of burnout during their ministry[5]. This is why they need people on their team to help them in the battle, and help them rest when needed. When Israel went to battle against the Amalekites, Moses stood on the hill with his staff raised high. Whenever Moses held the staff in the air, the Israelites had the lead and were winning the battle, but whenever he let down his hands the Amalekites gained the advantage.

"Moses' arms soon became so tired he could no longer hold them up. So Aaron and Hur found a stone for him to sit on. Then they stood on each side of Moses, holding up his hands. So his hands held steady until sunset." (Exodus 17:12)

Israel won the battle because two men served their leader by holding up his arms when he was fatigued. They chose not to complain in the midst of the battle. Instead, they served him by finding a rock for him to sit on and by lifting up their leaders' arms. They brought creative solutions to their leader's problem and helped win the battle. What tools, resources, or equipment can serve as your ministry leader's rock? How can you practically hold up their arms to help them achieve victory with less strain?

Our church opened a second campus and my Pastor would preach at the main campus for the 9 am service, then drive to our downtown campus to preach at the 10 am service, and drive back to preach at the 11 am service. He did this for several months, before we realized the strain it was causing. We decided to stream our 11 am service to the downtown location. This lightened the load for our Pastor significantly and we still got his message out.

Another example of this Kingdom Key practically playing out in our church was within our Communications team. At one point we did not have a system of communication to manage projects successfully. The pastors and ministry leaders had a difficult time getting their ministry promoted and getting information out about their ministry to the congregation successfully. We had a large church and with several ministry leaders, this was a major frustration for them. When I was placed in leadership over the Communications team, I immediately started to look for ways to streamline this broken process. We found a great project management software, and created web forms for projects submitted by other ministry leaders to ensure excellence of their projects. This eliminated frustration and unnecessary burdening to leaders on staff.

Most ministry leaders are pushing themselves to work 55-75 hours a week[6]. They are passionate to advance the Kingdom and are willing to put in whatever amount of time it takes to accomplish the mission. This is why it is vital that ministry leaders have people around them to guard against burnout. My Pastor is one of the hardest working individuals I have ever met. He is driven by holy purpose. One of the ways we protect him from burnout is by strongly encouraging him and his family to take times of rest throughout the year. He spends so much time pouring himself into shepherding the flock, he and his family need times of recharging and restoration. The staff and congregation have blessed him and his wife with surprise vacations. These trips bless the church as much as it blesses our Pastor because when he is given the time to be recharged and restored, he is more effective in his mission.

Even if your church body is unable to send your leaders on a vacation, make it a point to establish time during the year for every ministry leader to be refreshed. I promise you will find your church body has greater success for the Lord when your leaders are not burnt out. Whatever ministry you are involved in, be on the hunt for practical ways to make your leader's job easier. The rocks you provide could be the difference between victory and defeat in your ministry!

GUARD AGAINST DISCOURAGEMENT

Discouragement is one of the worst things people go through. It's an attack intended to cause people to quit. The lie that often comes with this spirit is "you're not making a difference." If you have ever encountered this feeling, you know how hopeless it can make you feel. This is why we need each other. The poll[7] referenced earlier stated 34% of ministry leaders battle discouragement and 43% are overstressed. This is why all ministry leaders need people around them who will encourage them. Jonathan was that for David,

> "Jonathan went to find David and encouraged him to stay strong in his faith in God." (1 Samuel 23:16)

Jonathan was David's armor-bearer and sought to encourage him concerning his faith. I want to challenge you to encourage your leader in their walk with God. Encourage them to stay true to the Word and not to deviate or compromise as pressures from the outside increase. Some leaders have become weak in their faith and have compromised the message of God to please the current culture, others simply give up due to the increasing pressures.

Encourage them when they are feeling down and out. Encourage them in their gifting and calling. Compliment them! If they are a speaker, let them know how their message impacted your life. If they are a leader in a ministry, compliment their leadership ability. If they are a worship leader, compliment them on the worship service. Your words have the power of life and death in them. Use them for life, to build people up.

> "Trustworthy messengers refresh like snow in summer. They revive the spirit of their employer." (Proverbs 25:13)

GUARD YOUR TRUST

The longer you serve your leader, the more vulnerable they will make themselves to you. You will begin to see things others don't see. You will see the humanity in them that other congregants will never see or know. You will see the frustrations and hardships they go through behind closed doors. You may not have asked for that, but because you serve it grants you access to them in a way only serving can. Rather than get comfortable, this should caution you to tread carefully all the more because they trust you. Remember the trap of familiarity and continue to honor your leader by guarding that trust. When I realized the extent of trust my leader had in me, I felt the fear of the Lord, because whenever there is trust, there is vulnerability. I never would want to compromise my Pastor's trust in any way. As relationships develop, trust is formed and trust is the reason David could be close to Saul yet not harm him, even when given the opportunity.

Earning and Guarding trust requires you to:

- Be a person of your word. If you say you're going to do something, be sure to do it.
- Protect your leader from as many attacks as you can.
- Be on time. This speaks volumes to a person's dependability.
- Be consistent with producing results. This shows you care for and value the ministry.
- Show support to other team members.
- Avoid gossip at all costs.

Trust isn't earned in a day, week, or even months, but in years of consistency. Once earned, be sure to do everything in your power to protect it. When you guard your integrity, God will guard you. "He is a shield to those who walk with integrity" (Proverbs 2:7 NLT).

*Trust is a valuable commodity, finding someone who
is faithful and trustworthy is a rarity.*

Daniel exemplified trustworthiness and faithfulness by living above reproach. His enemies were not able to find any issues of integrity or deceit in his life.

"Then the other administrators and high officers began searching for some fault in the way Daniel was handling government affairs, but they couldn't find anything to criticize or condemn. He was faithful, always responsible, and completely trustworthy." (Daniel 6:4 NLT)

He could not have received a higher compliment or description of his character. He was marked by integrity and one whom the king could trust, because of this he was promoted and prospered (Daniel 6:2, 28).

Lord, I want to guard my leader from attacks on every side. Prepare me to absorb spiritual attacks for my leader, draw me close and strengthen me so I am fit for battle. I want to be a person of trust, a person who can be confided in, a person of honor. Give me wisdom to know when to go to my leader, and wisdom to know when to only go to you. Let me be a support to my leader, let me hold them up when they are burning out Lord. Every time I guard my leader, I know I am ultimately serving you. In Jesus' name, amen.

KINGDOM KEY #11 PRAY FOR YOUR LEADERS

On Monday, November 25, 2019, at 5:45 PM, my pastor suffered a severe episode of cardiac arrest in our church parking lot. He laid there on the cement as the EMT's and paramedics compressed his heart over and over again. All present church body members surrounded them, praying for his survival, and declaring life over him. Finally, after thirty intense minutes of compressions and interceding as we had never done before, our Pastor's heart began to beat again. Paramedics quickly placed him in the ambulance and rushed him to the hospital. We found out later that 94% of people do not survive these types of cardiac arrest[1] events and were stunned to hear from the doctors that he had actually died there on the cement. God had truly performed a miracle!

The battle was far from over: multiple complications on that first night prompted doctors to warn us to "prepare for the worst." We refused to accept that, knowing in our spirits it was not time for our Pastor to leave the Earth yet. We covered him in prayer around the clock. We stationed ministry leaders in his room to pray and read the Word to him around the clock. We were there every minute the staff allowed us. Some of the hospital staff became annoyed at all the praying and worship music; one even remarked sarcastically, "We'll see if their prayer works."

The next four days were long and difficult as Pastor remained in the ICU in a medically induced coma. Though he had stabilized, doctors were very concerned about brain damage. I had to stand on this verse, "They do not fear bad news; they confidently trust the LORD to care for them" (Psalm 112:7). We knew in our spirits the doctors had to be wrong, why would God bring him back to life only to leave him brain dead? We knew we needed to contend for his full restoration and intercede on his behalf.

I spent that Friday evening in my Pastor's hospital room, praying and reading a few chapters of the Bible out loud to him. After I went home, I couldn't sleep. One thought was playing on repeat in my mind: the date Pastor had his cardiac arrest means something. I finally got my phone and looked up what day Monday was, it was 11/25. I started searching through my Bible to see if there was any significance and found John 11:25,

"Jesus told her, 'I am the resurrection and the life.
Anyone who believes in me will live, even after dying.'"

Jesus said these words after telling Mary that her brother Lazarus would live again. When I arrived at the hospital the next morning I found out that God had also spoken to my Pastor's wife that very morning, "I am the resurrection and the life." I excitedly shared with her what God revealed to me the night before and we were both greatly encouraged by God's confirmation as we started day five. We now call Day 5 the day of breakthrough. Pastor woke out of his coma, and gave us a thumbs up, indicating to doctors that he did not have brain damage. By the next afternoon, he was talking! After spending 16 days in the hospital, he was released and sent home.

This story is truly a testament to the power of our prayers when we pray for our leaders. It is imperative we intercede on their behalf. I know my pastor would have not survived that incident unless the saints prayed the way we did. We stood in the gap for him. There is nothing more powerful than praying for our leaders. Your ministry leader will go through difficult trials, hardships and storms, not to mention an increase of persecution as the days get closer to Christ's return. We see an example of this persecution in the early church when King Herod began hunting believers.

He had already killed the apostle James and had arrested Peter. The Church gathered together in unity, praying earnestly for Peter (Acts 12:5). It was that very night God sent an angel to miraculously deliver him. When Peter arrived at the house, the believers were still praying for him!

We are encouraged to pray for our leaders,

"Ask God to help them; intercede on their behalf, and give thanks for them. Pray this way for kings and all who are in authority." (1 Timothy 2:1-2)

I want to challenge you to pray daily for your leader. It's not the length of your prayer but the depth of your prayer; it is the sincerity of it. Do this daily, and it will have a tremendous impact on your leaders and bless them greatly. Hopefully, your leader will never have to go through what mine did, but you never know what trouble or struggle your daily prayer is protecting them from.

Take a moment and pray for them now. If you don't know what to pray, try something like this:

Lord, I know that my leader needs my prayers. I thank you for placing them in my life and ask that you help them in their ministry and calling. Strengthen them for the task. Give them peace in their mind. Bless them with health and rejuvenation in their body! Send your angels to surround them, and their family, and protect them wherever they go. Shield them from the attacks of the enemy. God, I ask that you give him/her a fresh fire for your Word and presence like never before and an even greater boldness to advance the kingdom. In Jesus' name, amen.

⊞ KINGDOM KEY #12
HONOR THE WORD

When Paul addresses the church, he stresses the importance of being battle ready to endure and withstand the last days. He tells us, "take the sword of the Spirit, which is the word of God" (Ephesians 6:17). It is imperative we understand that not only is the Word our spiritual nourishment, but it is our weapon. When Jesus was tempted in the wilderness, He fought temptation with the Word. You and I must know the Word and study the Word if we are going to conquer the battles and temptations of life. Paul tells his assistant Timothy:

"Do not waste time... Instead, train yourself to be godly. Physical training is good, but training for godliness is much better, promising benefits in this life and in the life to come." (1 Timothy 4:7-8)

We must train ourselves to be godly. You must become a person of discipline. Stop wasting time. Each day you must live with intentionality and laser focus. Put God first and sharpen your sword by spending quality time in the Word and His presence.

"All athletes are disciplined in their training. They do it to win a prize that will fade away, but we do it for an eternal prize. So I run with purpose in every step. I am not just shadowboxing. I discipline my body like an athlete, training it to do what it should. Otherwise, I fear that after preaching to others I myself might be disqualified." (1 Corinthians 9:25-27)

How much more devout, intentional and passionate should we be as believers than athletes? What we are doing is for an eternal prize. When we live this disciplined life like a champion athlete, we will not be disqualified for service but highly qualified. We will not forfeit our calling like many have, but we will champion God's call on our lives. Your talent and ability are not what prepares you for your calling, becoming a person of discipline prepares you. When you become a person of discipline, "Then each of you will control his own body and live in holiness and honor" (1 Thessalonians 4:4).

> *Honoring God's Word is the most important key*
> *to cultivating a life of honor.*

THE POWER OF THE WORD

Honoring God's Word is a crucial pillar in the Kingdom. I saved this key for last because I believe it will impact your successful fulfillment of all the prior keys. If you are going to have lasting honor and endure strong to the end, you must honor the Word in your life every day. You must know the Word and hide it in your hearts. I'm not saying you must attend Bible college before you start serving, however you must be in the Word daily, fixing your focus first on the Word and your relationship with God. Then, you will be better able to implement the Kingdom Keys.

Recently I spoke to a group of ministry leaders regarding the importance of honoring the Word. I challenged them to do a little self-examination. I explained that we all have priorities, we all have daily things we do consistently. I gave them a few minutes to make a list of things they do every day. When the time was up, most of the habits and regular preferences consisted of:

- Eating
- Shower
- Job
- Working out
- Brushing your teeth
- Checking social media
- Entertainment (tv, games, movies, etc.)

I asked them, "How would you rank these from most to least important?" They took a moment to write out their lists. Even though most had similar daily lists, the priority order varied. I then asked the question: "What number on your list is reading the Word?" Sounds of disappointment and shock immediately rumbled through the team. Reading the Word was not on their lists.

Several polls reveal that most Christians are not spending daily time in The Word[1]. A recent article stated that only 9% of Christian millennials read the Bible daily.[2] Why is this a fact among church-going believers? Simply put, we don't honor the Word. Most of us do not fully realize the value of the Word. Allow me to share one promise God gives to the believer that spends daily time in His Word:

"Study this book of instruction continually. Meditate on it day and night so you will be sure to obey everything written in it. Only then will you prosper and succeed in all you do." (Joshua 1:8)

Can you imagine that?
Daily reading will have such an epic impact on your life
that you will be successful in all that you do!

Once the Word gets before your eyes, it will penetrate your mind, it will penetrate your heart, it will penetrate your spirit. It will give you wisdom in all areas: ministry, finances, health, your workplace, family, relationships with people, and especially your relationship with God. Spending intimate time with the Lord daily is vital for your life. It is not an option; you must make the Word of God a daily priority in your life. When you fill yourself with the Word, you will walk in honor, obedience, and holiness. The Word of God is powerful, we are "washed by the cleansing of God's word" (Ephesians 5:25-26). Just like you take a shower daily for cleanliness and you eat daily for nourishment, the power of the Word cleanses us by renewing our mind and feeding us spiritually. The Word of God is what will help you cleanse yourself to become a vessel of honor.

"They delight in the law of the LORD, meditating on it day and night. They are like trees planted along the riverbank, bearing fruit each season. Their leaves never wither, and they prosper in all they do." (Psalm 1:2-3)

This verse was written 400 years after Joshua 1:8 and confirms what he said, "That those who delight in the Word day and night prosper in everything." Are you prospering in all avenues of your life? Could this be why the average Christian is not thriving and struggles in many areas? I want to challenge you to make the Word a priority in your life. Could you imagine what would happen if every believer spent quality time in the Bible daily? What would happen if God's Word became a staple in your day, and it was automatic? Beyond thriving in all you do, can you imagine what it would look like in your church if all the members of the Body were disciplined in reading the Word each day? How much more equipped would you be to serve your leaders and accomplish the work God has laid out for you?

INCREASE YOUR HUNGER FOR THE WORD

Many believers know Jesus died on the cross and forgave them of their sins. But that's all they know, they never understand the full experience. They don't walk in the fullness of their authority. The key to living the full experience of salvation is craving the Word of God. Look at what Peter said, "like newborn babies, you must crave pure spiritual milk so that you will grow into a full experience of salvation. Cry out for this nourishment" (1 Peter 2:2). The full experience is maturing and growing into what it means to be a vessel of honor. The key is to crave pure spiritual milk, which is God's Word. The New King James Version says, "As newborn babes, desire the pure milk of the word, that you may grow."

Strong's definition for desire is to intensely crave possession[3].

This is how we are to desire the Word. We are to intensely crave possession of it like babies. When that baby wants milk, nothing else will satisfy. Toys won't satisfy, nor will a new TV show suffice. There is only one thing that stops the crying. Milk. Nothing is as vital to that baby as milk. Milk is the baby's nourishment. Newborn babies need their milk every 2-3 hours, up to eight times a day! When you crave the Word like a baby needs milk, you will be like the psalmist who declared, "Oh, how I love your instructions! I think about them all day long" (Psalm 119:97).

I want to challenge you to make the Word a priority in your daily life. Here is how you can get started:

1. Pray: God, give me a greater passion and a desire for Your Word!

The psalmist's prayer was "Give me an eagerness for your laws rather than a love for money!" (Psalm 119:36). He was very specific and intentional in his prayer. He wasn't praying for a promotion at work, for God to give him a spouse, or anything monetary or materialistic. It was "give me an eagerness for your laws."

James tells us, "Yet you don't have what you want because you don't ask God for it. And even when you ask, you don't get it because your motives are all wrong—you want only what will give you pleasure" (James 4:2-3). The key to answered prayers is to ask God for the things He wants you to have. He wants you to be passionate about His Word. Therefore, start praying for an increase of passion for the Bible rather than praying for material things. "Turn my eyes from worthless things and give me life through your word." (Psalm 119:37).

2. Set a time and place to spend quality time with God daily.

Jesus got up early and went to an isolated place to spend time with God (Mark 1:35). As soon as you get up in the morning, get in the Word and welcome the Holy Spirit into your day. Do this before leaving to work or school. If mornings aren't optimal because of work and other schedule commitments, set another time that is exclusively God's time. Make feeding on God-breathed scripture even more important than physical food. Job said he treasured God's Word more than daily food (Job 23:12). Another important note is to pick an isolated place like Jesus did. This is imperative to guard your time with God from distractions.

At night, read the Word as you are lying in bed. Allow it to penetrate your mind and your spirit. I enjoy listening to the Bible on audio. Oftentimes, I like to set a 15-minute timer and listen while falling asleep at night.

"I honor and love your commands. I meditate on your decrees." (Psalm 119:48)

Lord, I see how important and valuable the Word is in my life and that you desire me to crave it. I want this to be a reality in my life. Forgive me for being distracted and drawn away to worldly things. Give me a greater passion and desire for Your Word. I want my heart to burn for You, your laws, and precepts. I want to experience the full salvation you have planned for my life. Turn my eyes from worthless things and give me life through Your Word. In Jesus' name, amen.

SECTION 4: SUMMARY

KEY #9) Give Double Honor: Our leaders deserve to be paid well for their work in the ministry. They deserve our financial support and gifts to encourage them. "Let the elders who rule well be counted worthy of double honor, especially those who labor in the word and doctrine. For the Scripture says, "You shall not muzzle an ox while it treads out the grain," and, "The laborer is worthy of his wages" (1 Timothy 5:17-18 NKJV).

KEY #10) Guard Your Leaders: Our leaders are going to face spiritual attacks, burnout, discouragement, and broken trust. We are charged with protecting them, absorbing some of their attacks, holding up their arms when tired, and honoring their trust in us. "He who guards his master will be honored" (Proverbs 27:18 ESV).

KEY #11) Pray for Your Leaders: Our leaders have a heavenly charge to disciple us and lead us in the way of the Lord. We are charged with interceding on their behalf before the Lord. By praying for them daily, we can have a tremendous impact on their lives and will bless them greatly. "Ask God to help them; intercede on their behalf, and give thanks for them. Pray this way for kings and all who are in authority" (1 Timothy 2:1-2).

KEY #12) Honor the Word: Keep your sword sharp. We cannot implement honor in our lives without honoring God's word and hiding it in our hearts. The Word changes us, challenges us, and transforms us. It must be a priority in our lives. "Study this book of instruction continually. Meditate on it day and night so you will be sure to obey everything written in it. Only then will you prosper and succeed in all you do" (Joshua 1:8 NLT).

SECTION 4: ACTION STEPS

1) Important Dates to honor your leader: Birthday, wedding anniversary, Pastors appreciation month and Christmas. If you don't know their birthday and wedding anniversary dates: Find out this week and put them on your calendar.

- If you serve a part of a ministry team, meet with the team and come up with creative ways you can honor your leader on these dates. Jot down activities, food, events and gifts you know your ministry leader enjoys. Try to come up with a variety of options. Be creative!

Remember, consistent double honor will provide on-going encouragement!

2) What tools, resources, or equipment can serve as your ministry leader's rock? How can you practically hold up their arms to help them achieve victory with less strain? Once you brainstorm these "arm lifters", begin to implement them and watch your leader be re-energized.

3) Add your leader to your daily prayer life. Set aside specific time to pray for them each day, set an alarm if you have to! Pray for God to strengthen and equip them for the heavenly burden they carry.

4) Surround your life with the Word of God (Deuteronomy 6:6-9).
   a. Set your Bible app to deliver the verse of the day to your phone
   b. Put verses on your walls, and bathroom mirrors.
   c. Leave your Bible open on your table, just by having it physically around you more, you will acknowledge it more and read it more.
   d. Set a 15-minute timer in bed at night and listen to the Word on audio. End your day with the good news, not the world's news.

RECOGNIZING REBELLION - PART 1

SECTION 5

⌐ THE SPIRITUAL
SICKNESS ⌐

The core of all sin is rebellion. Rebellion against God, His kingdom, or His delegated authority. Rebellion is a spiritual disease that many times removes people from fulfilling God's calling on their life before they even know it. Let's define rebellion[1]:

(re·bel·lion) resistance to or defiance of any authority
Synonyms: uprising, revolt, defiance, disobedience, insubordination.

In essence, rebellion is the opposite of honor. If honor calls us to esteem and respect, rebellion calls us to disparage, disrespect and dishonor. Rebellion to authority is on the rise, with growing resistance to church leaders as well as to government leaders. If things are going to improve, it must start with the church, the church sets the tone for the culture. This is why we, the church, must bring honor back! We must understand how serious rebellion is and why God hates it. Most people are completely unaware that, "He [God] is especially hard on those…who despise authority" (2 Peter 2:10).

When someone despises authority, they think little or nothing of the leaders God has placed in their lives: this is dishonor and rebellion. Peter tells us that God is especially hard on them. Life becomes difficult and the reason is that dishonor allows demonic spirits to operate in one's life. The Bible promises if you honor, life will go well for you (Exodus 20:12). The counterpart is also true, if you dishonor, life will not go well for you. Take notice of those people in your life that did not honor their parents, teachers, pastors, or bosses. Notice how their life goes haywire, they live in constant struggle.

> "'But those who still reject me are like the restless sea, which is never still but continually churns up mud and dirt. There is no peace for the wicked,' says, my God." (Isaiah 57:20-21)

For some reason, many Christians do not understand kingdom authority. They understand authority in the world outside the church: police officers, presidents, teachers and principals, coaches, even our workplaces with supervisors, managers, and CEOs. But in the church, some think of it as a social club. And that is precisely what the enemy wants. He wants us to think lightly of the church and not hold it in high regard with reverence. He wants us to treat what is holy as common (Ezekiel 22:26). If Christians view the church as a social club, we will not have proper respect toward the leadership and thereby withhold the proper honor. It's imperative we understand that dishonor leads us into rebellion, so that we can stay far away from it.

> "So anyone who rebels against authority is rebelling against what God has instituted, and they will be punished." (Romans 13:2)

REBELLION WILL REPLACE YOU

One of the strongest examples of dishonor leading to rebellion in the Bible is found in the life of King Saul. Israel was in a war against the Philistines, and the Philistine army far outnumbered Israel's. The Philistines had gathered 30,000 chariots, 6,000 horsemen, and more foot soldiers than could be counted. Israel's army stood at a meager 2,000 soldiers. The men of Israel, King Saul's army, started panicking and began hiding in caves and behind rocks. They were overwhelmed and trembled with fear. Keep in mind, they didn't have any weapons. Yes, I said no weapons.

> "So on the day of the battle none of the people of Israel had a sword or spear, except for Saul and Jonathan." (I Samuel 13:22)

Grossly outnumbered with only two weapons was a dangerous situation to be in. Saul had been instructed to wait for the prophet Samuel to arrive and offer a burnt offering to God, but it had already been seven days and Israel's army had dwindled down to 600 men. In a panic Saul decided, "We need to offer a burnt offering to God!" even though Samuel had not arrived yet. This was a duty reserved for Samuel to do as the prophet, not the king. King Saul had authority over all things civil, and Samuel had authority over all things sacred.

It is dangerous when you step out of your scope of authority into someone else's.

Saul, heavily feeling the pressure, and not trusting God to provide, proceeded with the burnt offerings. Just as Saul was finishing, Samuel arrived and, raising his voice said,

> "'How foolish!' Samuel exclaimed. 'You have not kept the command the Lord your God gave you. Had you kept it, the Lord would have established your kingdom over Israel forever. But now your kingdom must end, for the Lord has sought out a man after his own heart. The Lord has already appointed him to be the leader of his people, because you have not kept the Lord's command.'" (1 Samuel 13:13-14)

King Saul really thought he was honoring God by performing the burnt offering, but in reality he had taken the bait and believed the deception. He abandoned his faith in God's provision. He dishonored Samuel and that led to rebellion against God. The king assumed a role and a position that was not given to him; and therefore was replaced. It's interesting to note that just as Saul was finishing with the burnt offering, Samuel arrived. People often miss fulfilling their calling by trying to fulfill it in their own time. Many people, like King Saul, fall into sinful rebellion by trying to rush God's timing. I cannot tell you how often right before the miracle comes, the breakthrough happens, or the promotion is given, the enemy will start to apply pressure on you.

Pressure will reveal what's inside of you. What will be revealed, honor or dishonor?

When Samuel rebuked him, Saul started making excuses and blame-shifting. People of dishonor will always try to blame others for their disobedience. If they can shift the blame, they won't have to take responsibility for their actions. Unfortunately, Saul didn't repent, and this spirit of rebellion continued webbing deep into Saul's heart. We see two chapters later, he rebels against God again by not killing all the Amalekites.

"For rebellion is as the sin of witchcraft; And stubbornness is as iniquity and idolatry. Because you have rejected the word of the Lord, He also has rejected you from being king." (1 Samuel 15:23 NKJV)

Rebellion will replace you from ruling and reigning in the area of life you are called to! As tragic as the story of King Saul is, you and I should learn from it. We can learn from the devastating effects dishonor and rebellion have on a person's life, consequently guarding ourselves against the severity of its deception.

REBELLION WILL COST YOU THE PROMISED LAND

Most Christians know the story of Moses and the great deliverance out of Egypt. We know about the plagues, and we know about them crossing the Red Sea (which was an estimated 1.5 to 3 million people). We applaud and think that's such a great ending. Even most movies about Moses end after the Red Sea. I have found that fewer people know about how it really ended for the children of Israel.

When they departed from Egypt, their trip to the Promised Land was 240 miles. When you look at the pioneers that traveled across the United States a few hundred years ago, they covered between 15-20 miles a day on average[2]. Therefore, 240 miles would have taken about two weeks. But what happened between leaving Egypt to entering Canaan, the Promised Land?

Out of the 1.5 to 3 million people that were delivered from Egypt only two people from the original group ever made it to the Promised Land! Joshua and Caleb (see Numbers 14:26-33). The rest all died in the wilderness. So, what happened? You have to read Hebrews 3 and 4 for the short version as God reminds us of Israel's rebellion,

"While it is said: 'Today, if you will hear His voice, Do not harden your hearts as in the rebellion.' For who, having heard, rebelled? Indeed, was it not all who came out of Egypt, led by Moses? Now with whom was He angry forty years? Was it not with those who sinned, whose corpses fell in the wilderness?" (Hebrews 3:15-17 NKJV)

The Israelites dishonored their leaders and it cost them. They rebelled and it cost them. They constantly resisted what leadership was trying to accomplish. They had hidden agendas to usurp their leaders and no matter how hard Moses fought for unity there were those that did everything in their power to create division. This was tragic because these people had been delivered from slavery in Egypt. God did the miraculous to rescue them, yet rebellion corrupted them and hardened their hearts. Rebellion is nothing to overlook or sweep under the carpet. Their defiance angered God, and they died in the wilderness. The children of Israel missed their Promised Land.

Don't miss your Promised Land.

As we begin to examine the eight symptoms of this spiritual disease, notice how often the symptoms present themselves together, and often build on one another in increasing severity. If you recognize the symptoms of rebellion and dishonor in your life, address it early on and deal with it. Cancer is to the body what rebellion is to the spirit. Everyone knows how deadly cancer is and no one wants to be diagnosed when it is in Stage 4. Rebellion's consequences are as severe as cancer; it's important we recognize the signs early on.

Lord, I know sometimes I fall into rebellion in my life. I know that when I am entrenched in rebellion, I am opposing you. I am operating outside of honor and there will be consequences. I have seen rebellion's consequences before, and I don't want to live my life that way. Help me to discover and eliminate rebellion in my life Lord. I don't want to miss the Promised Land. I don't want to miss what you have planned for me. In Jesus' name, amen.

SYMPTOM #1
COMPLAINING

Complaining is one of the earliest signs of dishonor toward ministry leaders. This revelation shocked me because I never associated complaining as rebellious, but that's exactly what it is. We see this frequently through the children of Israel, "The whole community of Israel complained about Moses and Aaron" (Exodus 16:2).

Complaining is a verbalization of dissatisfaction with your current situation. Most people think if they can get enough listeners, they can change their situation. Complaining always starts with some form of dishonor, dissatisfaction, inconvenience, or hardship. I honestly never understood how big of a deal complaining was until I read this verse:

"Soon the people began to complain about their hardship, and the Lord heard everything they said. Then the Lord's anger blazed against them, and he sent a fire to rage among them, and he destroyed some of the people in the outskirts of the camp." (Numbers 11:1)

The children of Israel simply complained about their hardship and suffered tragic consequences for doing so. The reality is when we complain, we hurt the heart of God. When we complain, we are telling God that we are not grateful for all He has given us. We are not esteeming Him or His position of authority in our lives. Complaining within your ministry might sound like this:

- I wish we didn't have to do this.
- I hate setting up for youth ministry.
- I hate tearing down and cleaning up after service.
- I wish the pastor didn't preach so long.
- I don't like this worship song.
- I wish the pastor wouldn't take an offering.

What about complaining in your home life/work life?

- I wish we didn't have to eat leftovers.
- I wish I didn't have to wake up early for work.
- I hate how small our house is.
- My boss talks too long in meetings.
- I hate that we can't afford a vacation.

Do any of these statements sound familiar from those on your ministry team or members of your family? If you have people close to you that complain, be careful. That spirit spreads to those that are listeners. Complaining breeds negativity which leads to disunity. I want you to examine those that are in your inner circle. The children of Israel were affected by the foreign group traveling with them,

"Then the foreign rabble who were traveling with the Israelites began to crave the good things of Egypt. And the people of Israel also began to complain. 'Oh, for some meat!' they exclaimed. 'We remember the fish we used to eat for free in Egypt. And we had all the cucumbers, melons, leeks, onions, and garlic we wanted. But now our appetites are gone. All we ever see is this manna!'" (Numbers 11:4-6)

Wait a minute, the foreign rabble? These weren't the Israelites. They were traveling along with them. They started to crave things from Egypt which is a symbol of the world, and it caused the Israelites to complain and crave those too. I cannot stress this enough:

A complaining spirit will infect the whole team.

When you look back to Israel, they were complaining about their hardship, difficulties, and their manna. They were sick and tired of the manna. Here the Israelites were, rescued from slavery, protected by God Himself in the desert, food being delivered to them each day supernaturally and they were complaining! Have you ever heard people complain about food? I know I have been guilty of this many times before I saw this in scripture. The children of Israel couldn't resist the temptation to complain and look at how it affected their leader and even God,

"Moses heard all the families standing in the doorways of their tents whining, and the Lord became extremely angry. Moses was also very aggravated." (Numbers 11:10)

Complaining makes God angry
and aggravates your leaders.

Complaining and whining also negatively impacts your leaders by overburdening them with unnecessary negativity. We are not called to add burdens to them; we are called to lift up their arms and lighten their load. We are called to bring refreshing, strength, and encouragement to our leaders.

What happens next in the story is shocking. God sends them quail to eat from every direction. The people went out and gathered quail all day and all night and gathered even more the next day! Wow, they complained and got what they wanted. This is why people complain, after all, they want to be heard, they want to throw a pity party. The Lord sent quail, seems like a miracle and a blessing. I'm sure that's what they thought too, but take a look at what unfolds,

"But while they were gorging themselves on the meat—while it was still in their mouths—the anger of the Lord blazed against the people, and He struck them with a severe plague. So that place was called Kibroth-hattaavah (which means "graves of gluttony") because there they buried the people who had craved meat from Egypt." (Numbers 11:33-34)

What looked like a blessing turned out to be a curse. What seemed like a dream come true turned out to be a nightmare for the Israelites. Thousands of people died from complaining. I'm sure that just like you and I treat complaining lightly, not one of the Israelites thought their complaining was a big deal until it killed them. Those that perished never fulfilled the call that God had on their lives—all because of complaining about their hardship and food. In the New Testament, Paul reminds us of the Israelites and the price they paid for their complaining in the wilderness, let us learn from them,

"Now these things became our examples, to the intent that we should not lust after evil things as they also lusted… nor complain, as some of them also complained, and were destroyed by the destroyer. Now all these things happened to them as examples." (1 Corinthians 10:6, 10-11 NKJV)

***Complaining is the entry point of dishonor
and has a death sentence of rebellion attached to it.***

Lord, it is HARD to follow the command to do everything without complaining and arguing. Sometimes I am frustrated and tired, and I don't want to have a positive attitude. I want to complain. I want to whine like the Israelites. But God, I know this is a sin, it is rebellion. Father, help me to respond positively in all things. Help me to rejoice even in my harder tasks, knowing that I can have ultimate joy in ALL things because you saved me. In Jesus' name, amen.

SYMPTOM #2
CRITICIZING A LEADER

When individuals start criticizing those in leadership, they step on a slippery slope of dishonor and bring affliction on themselves through rebellion. Most are unaware of the dangers of criticism because its deceptive nature often masks itself as being discerning or spiritual. We can make a distinction between a spirit of criticism and a spirit of discernment by determining whether or not the statements are fueled by love.

Discernment is love. Criticism is loveless.

Be careful of those who look to find fault in people, or point out weaknesses in front of others. In the story of Miriam and Aaron, we see how God feels about a critical spirit especially when it is towards leadership,

"While they were at Hazeroth, Miriam and Aaron criticized Moses because he had married a Cushite woman. They said, 'Has the Lord spoken only through Moses? Hasn't he spoken through us, too?' But the Lord heard them. (Now Moses was very humble—more humble than any other person on earth.) So immediately the Lord called to Moses, Aaron, and Miriam and said, 'Go out to the Tabernacle, all three of you!' So the three of them went to the Tabernacle. Then the Lord descended in the pillar of cloud and stood at the entrance of the Tabernacle. 'Aaron and Miriam!' he called, and they stepped forward. And the Lord said to them,

'Now listen to what I say: 'If there were prophets among you, I, the Lord, would reveal myself in visions. I would speak to them in dreams. But not with my servant Moses. Of all my house, he is the one I trust. I speak to him face to face, clearly, and not in riddles! He sees the Lord as he is. So why were you not afraid to criticize my servant Moses?' The Lord was very angry with them, and he departed. As the cloud moved from above the Tabernacle, there stood Miriam, her skin as white as snow from leprosy."
(Numbers 12:1-10)

Here we see Miriam and Aaron both sought to find fault with Moses; they wanted to point out he had married a Cushite woman. But why did they criticize him? Why does anyone criticize or gossip about others? What is the purpose of finding fault in people or making it the aim to point it out? Critical people's motive is to tear someone else down, so they might be elevated in the eyes of others. Miriam and Aaron's motive is exposed in the second verse:

"They said, 'Has the Lord spoken only through Moses? Hasn't he spoken through us, too?' But the Lord heard them."
(Numbers 12:2)

They were comparing themselves with their leader, dishonoring him and tearing him down by criticizing him just to elevate themselves. Let me give you some examples of how people do this today. They say statements like:

- God doesn't only talk to my pastor; He speaks to me too.
- I walk with God closer than my pastor walks with God.
- Pastor's sermon was okay, he was wrong about that one point and could have said this point better.
- Why does he drive that car?

- Why does he live in that house?
- Is he really going to take another offering?
- Why are they wearing that?
- I'm not getting fed here.

Usually, these types of statements are said with a slant and a sarcastic tone, exposing their motive. These types of comments stem from a spirit seeking to elevate itself in the eyes of others and are often said behind the leader's back. Whenever you are speaking about others, ask yourself, "Is my motive to restore and build them up, or is it to tear them down and wound them?"

WHY WERE YOU NOT AFRAID TO CRITICIZE MY SERVANT?

God asked Miriam and Aaron, "Why were you not afraid to criticize my servant Moses?" (Numbers 12:8). This tells us there should be a reverence or a holy fear within our hearts when it comes to criticizing God's leaders. If we feared criticizing our leaders, we would think twice before saying anything negative about them.

God does not take criticizing ministry leaders lightly. We see this in a story with Elisha. He encounters several boys who begin mocking and making fun of him. This brought quick judgement on them as two bears came out of the woods and mauled forty-two boys (2 Kings 2:23-35). They criticized God's servant and paid the price with their lives and the lives of many others.

As believers, it is important we know the things God loves and the things He hates. Solomon tells us, "There are six things which the LORD hates, Yes, seven which are an abomination to Him... one who spreads strife among brothers" (Proverbs 6:16, 19 NASB). The Lord absolutely hates when someone stirs up conflict or brings division among His family.

Criticism is in direct opposition to honor. This is precisely why criticism is so threatening. When Paul was summoned to stand before the Jewish High Council, he illustrated again that God will not tolerate criticism of a leader.

> "Gazing intently at the high council, Paul began: 'Brothers, I have always lived before God with a clear conscience!' Instantly Ananias the high priest commanded those close to Paul to slap him on the mouth. But Paul said to him, 'God will slap you, you corrupt hypocrite! What kind of judge are you to break the law yourself by ordering me struck like that?'" (Acts 23:1-3)

Strong rebuke! We all love Paul, we love his boldness, passion, intensity, and conviction. Paul is one of our heroes, but before we get excited and say, "there you go Paul, let them have it!" read the next verse,

> "Those standing near Paul said to him, 'Do you dare to insult God's high priest?' 'I'm sorry, brothers. I didn't realize he was the high priest,' Paul replied, 'For the Scriptures say, 'You must not speak evil of any of your rulers.'" (Acts 23:4-5)

This is profound because Paul crossed the line of dishonor into criticism, but as soon as he was aware of it, he humbled himself and apologized. Remember, honor + humility = a servant's heart ready for ministry. This kind of rapid humility would solve many church issues and prevent situations from escalating.

I knew two ministry leaders who gossiped and slandered their pastor to mutual friends. When the pastor had found that these conversations had taken place, he called them in to address the situation. Rather than humble themselves and apologize, they became proud and defiant and stormed out of the office. Their lack of humility and honor destroyed the servant's heart within them, and they lost their ministry that day. Whenever you realize you've crossed the line of dishonor, quickly humble yourself and sincerely apologize. If you don't, you'll find yourself reaping the consequences of rebellion faster than you can imagine.

ACCOUNTABILITY

In my early twenties, I was serving at a church and became critical of my senior pastor. I didn't agree with certain ministry decisions or lifestyle choices, and I allowed my heart to become critical of him. Once, while in a conversation with my friend, I began venting about my disapproval of our senior pastor, and even though some things I was saying may have been right, it was filtered through criticism—the wrong motive. My friend immediately checked me and said, "That's our pastor, we can't talk about him like that. If he's wrong, God will address it and deal with him." My words were not only rebellious, but I was also not treating my pastor with the honor his position deserves. It's important that we invite other believers into our lives to hold us accountable, especially in the area of criticism. Ask those close to you or those involved in your ministry to keep your heart in check if they hear you begin to criticize your leaders.

I thank God for my friend keeping me accountable, rather than entertaining the criticism. You can be sharing facts, but it all comes down to the motive. We see the pure heart of a prophet in Samuel. He saw the rise and downfall of King Saul; he saw the good, the bad, and the ugly. Yet look at his heart:

"Then the Lord said to Samuel, 'I am sorry that I ever made Saul king, for he has not been loyal to me and has refused to obey my command.' Samuel was so deeply moved when he heard this that he cried out to the Lord all night." (1 Samuel 15:10-11)

Before being critical of someone, especially your God-appointed leaders, examine your motives and ask, have you cried out on their behalf, and have you interceded in prayer for them? Is your heart sincerely broken for them? Or are you happy or pleased when you see judgment coming on them? As Samuel watched the downfall of Saul, "Samuel never went to meet with Saul again, but he mourned constantly for him." (1 Samuel 15:35) This is the true heart of a prophet. A broken heart for those that fall, not one of rejoicing. James tells us,

> "Don't speak evil against each other, dear brothers and sisters. If you criticize and judge each other, then you are criticizing and judging God's law." (James 4:11)

Criticism is the match that
sparks the flame of destruction.

DO NOT TOUCH GOD'S ANOINTED

"Do not touch My anointed ones, And do My prophets no harm."
(1 Chronicles 16:22 NKJV)

This statement was from God himself, not a corrupt king or leader in power trying to control people. Every one of us should have a fear of the Lord when it comes to dishonoring a leader and touching those who God has anointed in places of authority. King Uzziah was a godly leader who didn't guard himself against pride. This led to him rebelling against his spiritual authority, the priest, and the consequences were severe. While he was raging at the priests in a fit of uncontrolled anger, God struck him with leprosy (see 2 Chronicles 26:19).

David understood the principle "Do not touch the Lord's anointed". When Saul became extremely jealous of David to the point of wanting to kill him; David was forced to flee for his life. On two different occasions, David had the opportunity to kill him and yet spared his life both times (1 Samuel 24 & 26). During the first occasion, David's men were urging him to kill Saul while he was relieving himself in the cave. David's response was:

"He said to his men, 'The Lord forbid that I should do this to my lord the king. I shouldn't attack the Lord's anointed one, for the Lord himself has chosen him.'" (1 Samuel 24:6)

During the second incident, Saul was asleep when David and Abishai snuck into the camp and got close to him. Abishai said to David, "I'll kill Saul for you," and David responded,

"'No!' David said. 'Don't kill him. For who can remain innocent after attacking the Lord's anointed one?'" (1 Samuel 26:9)

Four times in chapter 26, David mentions Saul as the Lord's anointed. Keep in mind, Saul was proud, arrogant, and crossed the line by performing the duties set apart for only Samuel. It had been prophesied that God was tearing Saul's kingdom from him. He was a murderer, responsible for the killing of 86 priests, and was now seeking to kill David. Why would David give him such honor? David deeply understood the principles of kingdom authority and that Saul was still in an authority position. David understood that honoring his authority, no matter how corrupt, would honor God and ultimately bring David honor. He knew the impact of dishonor would bring destruction down on himself. David did not verbally or physically attack the Lord's anointed in any way, and he would later receive the reward for his honor.

Lord, My heart can be proud and critical of others. There are times I find myself critiquing the leaders you've placed in my life. There are times I gossip about them to others; times I think I know better than they. Forgive me Lord. The leaders in my life are there because YOU chose them. They are part of your master plan. They are your anointed ones and I am charged with honoring them. Humble my heart Lord, remind me to pray for my leaders, rather than tear them down. Help me remember that the ultimate goal we ALL should have is the furthering of Your Kingdom. In Jesus' name, amen.

SYMPTOM #3
NEGATIVE ATTITUDE

A negative attitude is a manifestation of dishonor. God told Moses to send men out to explore the land of Canaan, the land God had promised them. After they explored the land, some within the group gave Moses a negative report filled with doubt, fear, and unbelief because of the giants they saw there.

> "But Caleb tried to quiet the people as they stood before Moses. 'Let's go at once to take the land,' he said. 'We can certainly conquer it! But the other men who had explored the land with him disagreed. 'We can't go up against them! They are stronger than we are!' So they spread this bad report about the land among the Israelites." (Numbers 13:30-32)

The pessimists went and spread a negative report to all the others, telling everyone about the giants and how they seemed like grasshoppers next to them. This brought others under a spirit of fear, who started to protest against Moses and Aaron. Joshua and Caleb pleaded with the people not to rebel against the vision and not to fear, for the Lord would give them the victory. Unfortunately, the negativity had already spread and affected the entire camp. The people believed the negative report so strongly that they talked about stoning Joshua and Caleb for disagreeing. Someone with a negative attitude will always try to silence the voices of those that want to advance the Kingdom.

Does this happen today? Yes, it does.

- When a pastor wants to buy a new building to increase opportunities for evangelism, you'll hear things like, "This is not a good choice financially, he's going to bankrupt the church."

- When a leader wants to start a new ministry, "We should be spending the money on this other ministry, we should do this other ministry for the homeless."

- When a pastor wants to do outreach or production, "We are overloaded with work, we can't add another thing to our plate."

- When a pastor wants to change the name of the church to be more relevant and modern, "The old name had so much history. He's taking us away from our roots."

When your pastor has a vision for the church, and you disagree, do not spread an adverse report to other church members on why you think the church shouldn't do it. You are in opposition to authority if your pastor is pushing the gas pedal to move forward and you are trying to push the brakes. That is not your decision to make unless you are in the driver seat or one of the decision-makers.

NEGATIVITY DELAYS PROGRESS

As I mentioned before, I spent several years as the ministry lead for the communications team at our church. I remember feeling like our ministry should have been far more effective than it was. We had a relatively large group of staff, interns and volunteers, but for some reason, projects were taking longer than they should have. Finally, it came to light that several individuals were engaging in the rebellion through gossip and having a negative attitude. When I would roll out a project, they would spread bad reports without my knowledge. Rather than jumping in the boat, grabbing an oar, and rowing, they were too busy spreading negativity, poking holes in the bottom of the boat so that we were always almost sinking. I remember it felt like the spiritual equivalent of driving with a flat tire.

Don't be the flat tire on your team,
flat tires get fixed, or they get replaced.

I found out who the individuals were that had been spreading negativity and I addressed them strongly. There was repentance and breakthrough in our team. Unfortunately, we had to let one go because he wouldn't repent and engage in restoration. After that, the team culture significantly improved and began to thrive. There was nothing we couldn't accomplish as a team. Anything we were dreaming of, we achieved with ease. There was truly a divine grace that came over our team because we were in unity and the negative and divisive spirit had been removed.

Keep in mind, rebellion's agenda is to slow down and even stop Kingdom progression. I call it a spirit of delay. This can come in many ways, but the most common I have seen is when someone:

- Makes things harder than they need to be.
- Finds reasons we should not be working on the prioritized goal.
- Constantly makes excuses.
- Has a negative attitude.
- Has an employee mindset, a clock in clock out mentality. Someone with a ministry mindset is willing to go the extra mile to get the job done.

If you see these symptoms in your life, repent to God and repent to your ministry leader. Watch as God pours His grace over you and your team.

WHAT IF I FEEL MY LEADER IS DRIVING THE MINISTRY IN A WRONG DIRECTION? IS THERE ANYTHING I CAN DO?

Yes, absolutely! You can go to your pastor or leader and share the genuine concerns you have. There have been times over the years that I have shared concerns with my senior Pastor. He appreciated it each time. There are also times he has asked my opinion on ministry plans and endeavors. When he asks, I know that I am responsible to give an honest opinion based on the knowledge and ministry experiences I have. I also know it is his responsibility to make the call, not mine. My responsibility is to treat him with honor, regardless of the situation.

Before going to your leader, ask yourself these three questions:

1) Are You Acting in a Spirit of Honor?

"Never speak harshly to an older man, but appeal to him respectfully as you would to your own father." (1 Timothy 5:1)

There is so much we can learn from this verse. If you always address ministry leaders with this attitude you will maintain and protect your honor. I have also learned that what you share is more likely to be well-received when you approach your leader with this respectful attitude, rather than with pride or arrogance.

2) Are You Bringing Solutions?

Remember, most people only bring problems to their leader. Stating the obvious issues is entirely unhelpful unless you have potential solutions. David went before King Saul when they were facing the problem of going against Goliath and the Philistines. In this particular situation, the king did not have a solution. David went before the king and said, "I'll go fight him!" He brought the solution and was willing to take care of the problem himself. He took ownership. David's willingness to participate not only in providing the solution but carrying it out brought honor to Saul's kingdom and ultimately God.

3) Have You Earned the Right to Share Your Opinion?

Throughout my years of ministry, I have seen people who don't serve or give consistently, and they want to share their opinion about the direction of the church. Their words fall flat. However, I can surely tell you those who served faithfully in the ministry are the ones whose voices carry the most weight. Those who serve have proven themselves faithful and trustworthy have earned the right to share their opinion because their hearts, time, and resources are invested in the ministry of the church. Those in the Bible that served exceptionally well were respected by their leaders. Their ideas and solutions were well received:

- Esther served king Xerxes
- David served king Saul
- Joseph served Pharaoh
- Daniel served king Nebuchadnezzar
- Nehemiah served king Artaxerxes

Each had a voice in their sphere of influence because their words were backed with a lifestyle of honor.

I want to encourage you even if your leader decides to make a decision that you don't necessarily agree with, submit and support them with a positive attitude. If you have ever played sports, you understand the power of unity. If a quarterback calls a play, it is best everyone on the team runs the play with 100% effort whether they think it is the best play or not at that moment. Miracles happen when everyone gives 100%, running the play in unity. Keep in mind, Jesus submitted to the authority of His mother when asked to perform the miracle at the wedding of Cana. Jesus told her it was not yet His time, yet Mary insisted. Jesus submitted to her authority as his mother respectfully and performed His first miracle. (see John 2:1-12) God blesses honor and unity. Let God be God. He is more concerned about His church than we are. He will not hold you responsible if your leader makes a bad decision, but He will hold you accountable if you are dishonorable.

Lord, I do not want to cause division in the body. I do not want to be hitting the brakes while my leader has their foot on the gas pedal. May I be like Caleb and Joshua instead of those who spread a bad report about the land. They were the only two Israelites who made it to the Promised Land. They gave a good report. They trusted their leader. They operated with powerful positivity that I want to radiate. In Jesus' name, amen.

SYMPTOM #4 DESIRING A NEW LEADER

I have seen two unhealthy variations of desiring a new leader in the church today. People desire a new leader that will allow them to live in sin. These individuals do not want to give up their sinful lifestyles to truly follow Jesus. The other unhealthy pursuit I have seen is when people are looking for new leaders to promote them. They will go from church to church desiring to be recognized or discovered. Both motives are driven from a fleshly ambition. Both are symptoms of dishonor that has led them to rebellion.

WANTING A LEADER THAT WILL TAKE THEM BACK TO THE WORLD

When you examine the children of Israel right after the account of the men spreading negativity, their bad report affected the entire community. All the families began crying, and the Bible says they wept all night and continued complaining. "Then they plotted among themselves, 'Let's choose a new leader and go back to Egypt!'" (Numbers 14:4). The negativity impacted the community to the point of mutiny against God's appointed leader.

Rather than accomplish Moses' vision, they wanted to choose a new leader. This is not uncommon, when an individual has a spirit of rebellion. Rather than submit to their authority, they want to find someone who will give them what they want.

If you only submit when you want to,
it's not real submission.

The children of Israel wanted a leader to take them back to Egypt. I was blown away when I read this because Egypt was a place of bondage and idol worship. They wanted to go back to where they had been delivered from. Just like the Egyptians, in the last days "Christians" will want a leader who will take them back into secularism. A leader who will take them back to their familiar place of bondage, sin, worldliness, and idolatry. They want a watered-down gospel.

> "For a time is coming when people will no longer listen to sound and wholesome teaching. They will follow their own desires and will look for teachers who will tell them whatever their itching ears want to hear." (2 Timothy 4:3)

Here are some statements you might hear when someone is displaying this symptom:

- "I don't think we need to preach about sin, let's not offend any one."
- "We don't need to talk about holiness, after all holiness is old fashioned."
- "Let's have a little fun, let's not be legalistic." The fun they're talking about is compromising.

Those who have fallen into rebellion will want to find a pastor or leader who makes them feel good about their lack of transformation, one who condones their sin. They do not want accountability in their life. The purpose of your pastor is not to make you feel good. Your pastor's role is to refine and disciple you. Look at what Paul told the young pastor Timothy:

"Preach the word of God. Be prepared, whether the time is favorable or not. Patiently correct, rebuke, and encourage your people with good teaching." (2 Timothy 4:2)

WANTING A LEADER WHO WILL PROMOTE YOU

Some people make up their mind what they are going to do, then go to their leaders in the hopes they agree. They feel they are ready to move up in ministry, step into leadership, and obtain a promotion. These individuals do not go to their leaders to seek their input and leadership on the matter; they go to tell the leaders what they feel God has led them to do. Telling your leader to promote you is not true submission.

A few years ago, I met a young man who was passionate for the Lord, the Bible and holiness. He was serving at his church in the youth ministry, as well as attending a Christian University. Another church in the city had expressed interest in him and offered him a youth pastor position. He went to his pastor, asking him for advice and counsel. The pastor didn't feel it was the right move for him and thought it was premature. This young man told him, "Well I already accepted the position." The pastor thought, "Why did you even ask me what I thought?"

This young man went on to do what he wanted to do and became the youth pastor at that church. A year later, he was no longer a youth pastor there nor in any ministry role. Unfortunately, he and his wife have since divorced. The sad reality is his previous pastor saw great potential in him, yet he decided to rush the process. He wanted a leader who would promote him in his own time, and rebelling against wise counsel cost him.

Most people want a motivational speaker
and not a pastor.

After Moses announced that the children of Israel were denied the Promised Land, they refused to submit to him once again and decided to take matters into their own hands. They got their weapons and were determined to fight for the Promised Land. Moses warned them not to go because God was not with them. He warned them: "'If you go ahead on your own, you will be crushed by your enemies. This is what I told you, but you would not listen. Instead, you again rebelled against the Lord's command and arrogantly went into the hill country to fight'" (Deuteronomy 1:42-43).

The Israelites tried to go around Moses and the Lord's directive to achieve their Promised Land, and as a result, "Then the Amorites who lived in that hill country came out against you and chased you as bees do and beat you down in Seir as far as Hormah. 45 And you returned and wept before the Lord, but the Lord did not listen to your voice or give ear to you" (Deuteronomy 1:44-45 ESV).

The Israelites were ready to move forward and achieve their end goal. That young man was ready to achieve the next level in ministry. Neither honored their leader's wisdom and input. Neither achieved what they were desiring. Both suffered because of their rebellion. Be careful not to circumvent your leader in an attempt to achieve promotion or your own agenda and goals. It will certainly result in unfavorable consequences.

Lord, I confess that it would be easier to have a leader who will let me sit in my sin. It would be easier to have a leader who I could push around, demand a promotion from, and behave as I please. I also know that under that leader I would not grow at all. I would remain entangled in my sin; honestly no better off than before I came to know you. I want to desire rebuke, course correction, and tough love from my leader. I want to desire accountability, so I can become holy. I don't want to be promoted of my own volition. I want to serve you SO faithfully that you prompt my leader to increase my responsibilities for your Kingdom. I want to operate under righteous kingdom authority. In Jesus' name, amen.

SECTION 5: SUMMARY

The Spiritual Sickness: The core of all sin is rebellion against God, His Kingdom, or His delegated authority. When we dishonor authority, we fall prey to rebellion's consequences. Rebellion will replace you and cost you the Promised Land. "So anyone who rebels against authority is rebelling against what God has instituted, and they will be punished" (Romans 13:2).

SYMPTOM #1) Complaining: A verbalization of dissatisfaction with your current situation. A complaining spirit will infect your whole team, anger God, and aggravate your leaders. "Moses heard all the families standing in the doorways of their tents whining, and the Lord became extremely angry. Moses was also very aggravated" (Numbers 11:10).

SYMPTOM #2) Criticizing a Leader: Be careful not to look for ways to find fault in people or point out weaknesses in front of others. Do not use criticism of your leader to elevate yourself. "Don't speak evil against each other, dear brothers and sisters. If you criticize and judge each other, then you are criticizing and judging God's law" (James 4:11).

SYMPTOM #3) Negative Attitude: Do not be the flat tire on your team, constantly cutting down ideas and ministries. Such a report creates judgement and division within the body. "Watch out for people who cause divisions…Stay away from them. Such people are not serving Christ our Lord; they are serving their own personal interests" (Romans 16:17-18).

SYMPTOM #4) Desiring a New Leader: Do not wish for a leader that will allow you to remain sinful in the world or promote you according to your own timelines and purposes. This will only lead to your ruin. "If you go ahead on your own, you will be crushed by your enemies. This is what I told you, but you would not listen. Instead, you again rebelled against the Lord's command and arrogantly went into the hill country to fight" (Deuteronomy 1:42-43).

SECTION 5: ACTION STEPS

1. Ask your ministry leader to tell you if they ever hear you complain or come across as negative, let them know you never want to be that person.

2. Choose a godly friend that you spend a considerable amount of time with and trust with matters of accountability. Let them know if they ever hear you criticizing a leader, complaining or being negative, to bring it to your attention. Give them the freedom to rebuke you.

3. Ask God to help you embrace and even love correction. Memorize these two verses:

    "To learn, you must love discipline; it is stupid to hate correction." (Proverbs 12:1)

    "If you ignore criticism, you will end in poverty and disgrace; if you accept correction, you will be honored." (Proverbs 13:18)

4. Take a moment and make a list of:

    What are you grateful for about your leader?
    How have they impacted your life?
    What do they do well as a leader?
    What do you love about them?

RECOGNIZING REBELLION - PART 2

SECTION 6

SYMPTOM #5
PRIDEFUL ATTITUDE

Pride always leads to dishonor and rebellion against leadership in one way or another. When someone challenges their leaders due to a prideful spirit, it is evident in their tone and attitude. They no longer speak with the utmost respect or love. People who are entrenched in the sin of pride believe they know more than their leader, can do better than their leader, are better suited for leadership than their leader. Isn't this what Lucifer did in heaven? He was full of pride and provoked a rebellion. How in the world did Lucifer think he could defeat God? He was just an angel going against the all-powerful God. This is the danger and deception of pride:

Pride makes you think you're stronger than you really are.

If we look back at the children of Israel, we see this with Korah. He conspired with others and incited a rebellion, causing 250 people to rise up against Moses (Numbers 16:1-2). What the people were accusing Moses of, they themselves were guilty of! They raised their voices at Moses,

"'You have gone too far! The whole community of Israel has been set apart by the Lord, and he is with all of us. What right do you have to act as though you are greater than the rest of the Lord's people?'" (Numbers 16:3)

They were literally accusing Moses of pride when in actuality they were the ones with an overinflated self-importance. Their words against Moses were merely a reflection of their own hearts. We are told in Numbers 12:3 that Moses was the most humble man on the face of the earth. Moses responded, telling them they had crossed the line and were *actually* rebelling against God. (Numbers 16:11) This is what most fail to realize in the moment of rebellion: pride blinds us from seeing who we are really opposing. When we rebel, resist, or dishonor those in authority, we are opposing God, and we will suffer consequences. (Romans 13:2)

PRIDE ON JESUS' TEAM

Be on the lookout for pride in your own life and on the team you serve with. It doesn't matter what ministry team you serve on, whether it's the worship team, usher team, or children's ministry. It doesn't matter if you are a volunteer or a paid staff member, pride grieves the heart of God. Jesus had to address this among His team and arguably at the worst possible time, the Last Supper.

> "Then they began to argue among themselves about who would be the greatest among them." (Luke 22:24)

This is the night of Jesus' betrayal, the historic night that changed everything, and the disciples are arguing about which one of them is the greatest, could you even fathom this situation?!? This is the last thing you expect to happen at such a somber moment. It's the Last Supper and here they are fighting about who is the greatest disciple! Jesus interrupted them and directly addressed Peter, "'Satan has asked to sift each of you like wheat'" (Luke 22:31).

That same night Jesus washed their feet, displaying ultimate humility and true servant leadership. The night before Jesus left to win the battle of

the grave, He humbled himself in servanthood. In response to His disciples arguing about which one of them was the greatest, Jesus got down on
His knees and washed their feet. His actions should speak volumes to us
about the importance of refraining from pride. The Son of God never focused on elevating Himself, He focused on serving others. (John 13:12-17)

THE COST OF PRIDE

The story of King Saul is one of the most tragic stories in the Bible. Saul
became the first King of Israel because he was humble. In the end, he lost
his kingship because his heart became inflamed with pride.

"Is it not true that even though you were small (insignificant) in
your own eyes, you were made the head of the tribes of Israel?
And the Lord anointed you king over Israel,"
(1 Samuel 15:17 AMP)

King Saul's pride cost him his kingdom and his position of authority.

"Pride goes before destruction, a haughty spirit before a fall."
(Proverbs 16:18)

Jesus taught a parable that detailed the steep price of pride.

"Two men went to the Temple to pray. One was a Pharisee, and the
other was a despised tax collector. The Pharisee stood by himself
and prayed this prayer: 'I thank you, God, that I am not like other
people—cheaters, sinners, adulterers. I'm certainly not like that
tax collector! I fast twice a week, and I give you a tenth of my income.' But the tax collector stood at a distance and dared not even
lift his eyes to heaven as he prayed. Instead, he beat his chest in

sorrow, saying, 'O God, be merciful to me, for I am a sinner.' I tell you, this sinner, not the Pharisee, returned home justified before God. For those who exalt themselves will be humbled, and those who humble themselves will be exalted." (Luke 18:10-14)

Pride is a sin of the spirit and can be difficult to detect. Its power to throw us into rebellion is enormous. If someone was drunk or having an affair, it would be fairly easy to see because those are sins that occur visibly outside the body, a sin of the flesh. Sins of the spirit are much harder to detect, which is why we need to be mindful of this rebellious spirit creeping in. The Pharisee could see the sin in everyone else's life but could not see the snare in his own life! This blindness condemned his soul. "I tell you, this sinner, not the Pharisee, returned home justified before God" (v14). Pride cost the Pharisee his own life. What might this symptom of rebellion cost you in your own life if it grows undetected?

"Pride ends in humiliation, while humility brings honor."
(Proverbs 29:23)

In the blind spot of pride
lies the path to destruction.

SYMPTOM #6 BLAMING YOUR LEADER

Rebellion was seen in the children of Israel when they blamed Moses and Aaron for the difficulties in the wilderness (Numbers 20:3). Most of the difficulty they experienced they brought on themselves. It was never God's intention for them to wander as long as they did in the wilderness; they prolonged the journey.

Oftentimes people will blame their leaders because they feel like their leaders are holding them back from their destiny.

When this occurs, hearts become contaminated with dishonor and leaders begin to be viewed as the enemy. This path of rebellion is exactly what the devil wants to see, this path leads straight to dishonor. When you blame a leader, you are idolizing them by saying they are in control of your life, rather than God. Our leaders have been appointed by God and as such they can make decisions that affect what happens to us, but only to the extent that God allows it. God is ultimately in control, so blaming your leader paints a power over them that they do not possess. It is rebellion and sin to blame your leaders. They are not God, and they do not have the power to stop your destiny or your dreams from coming to pass.

One of my favorite scriptures in the Bible is when Joseph was raised to power and is addressing his brothers nearly 20 years after they sold him into slavery. He said to them, "You intended to harm me, but God intended it all for good. He brought me to this position so I could save the lives of many people" (Genesis 50:20). He never blamed those who betrayed him. Instead, Joseph honored God and declared He was behind the scenes the entire time, orchestrating the details of his life. He knew that God brought him to that specific time, place, and position. When Joseph revealed his identity to his brothers, he told them not to worry or be angry at themselves for what they had done to him and reminded them three times it was God who sent him there (Genesis 45:5, 7-8).

The devil cannot change God's path for you, nor can a corrupt leader. The devil is fully aware of his limitations and this is why he is after your honor. The devil knows that if he can get you to dishonor your leaders by blaming him, you are ultimately dishonoring God. Keep in mind God is always behind the scenes working out His purposes for His children who love Him (Romans 8:28).

FEELING MISTREATED

I want to let you know that as you serve in ministry, there may be times you are mistreated under leadership. This does not necessarily mean you quit, or leave the church. There are too many people with a call of God on their lives who hold on to an offense and years pass, time to work for the Kingdom is wasted. This is exactly what the devil wants.

My wife and I have gone through several seasons where we were mistreated as we have both worked in the secular field and in ministry. We have both been under healthy leadership and unhealthy leadership. I'm sure you can relate. I want to encourage you that God sees everything you go through and He will work everything out. This passage has brought me significant encouragement during the times I was treated wrongly.

"Submit to your masters with all respect. Do what they tell you— not only if they are kind and reasonable, but even if they are cruel." (1 Peter 2:18)

Did you notice the last part? Even to leaders that are cruel! This was shocking to me, but consider other translations:

"Not only to the good and gentle, but also to the harsh." NKJV
"Not only to the good and gentle but also to the unjust." ESV

There are times our leaders are going to be harsh, unjust, or cruel. There are times your leaders will act out in the flesh and say things they should not say. They may hurt your feelings or come across rudely. When this happens, it is crucial you handle this correctly. I cannot emphasize enough that a high level of self-control is necessary. Dealing with mistreatment is one of the most challenging tests you will go through and will determine if you are rewarded or not. Don't retaliate, but instead allow God to deal with your leader. You don't need to worry about them, they are not under your authority. God will not hold you responsible for what they do. He will deal with them and judge them. He is looking at your response and how you handle the situation.

When you defend yourself,
you get in the way of God defending you.

You may be wondering, how does honoring leaders even when they treat me wrong, help me grow? Look at the rest of the passage in 1 Peter,

"For God is pleased when, conscious of his will, you patiently endure unjust treatment. Of course, you get no credit for being patient if you are beaten for doing wrong. But if you suffer for doing good and endure it patiently, God is pleased with you. For God called you to do good, even if it means suffering, just as Christ suffered for you. He is your example, and you must follow in his steps. He never sinned, nor ever deceived anyone. He did not retaliate when he was insulted, nor threaten revenge when he suffered. He left his case in the hands of God, who always judges fairly." (1 Peter 2:19-23)

God is pleased when you and I patiently endure unjust treatment. The New King James Version translation says, "This is commendable." This is an opportunity for you to follow in Jesus' footsteps. It is through these trials you have the opportunity to handle these situations correctly and please the heart of God. It is through these circumstances that the fruits of the Spirit will radiate out of your life, if you choose a path of honor.

I went through a trial in high school when I worked at a fast food restaurant. My boss, who was a professing Christian, was scheduling me to work shifts, and then the morning of would call me and cancel my shift. This went on for several weeks. I was eventually let go from the restaurant which confused me and hurt deeply. My heart was broken because I knew I did nothing wrong, and I really cared for my boss. I remember praying to God on his behalf that night, with tears in my eyes that God would have mercy on him. He lost his company a couple of months later. God will deal with those in authority. It is your job to fully trust God and do what Jesus did, "He did not retaliate… He left his case in the hands of God, who always judges fairly" (v23).

Hagar was a servant of Abraham's household and served Sarai. There was a time when Sarai put Hagar in a bad situation with her husband and as a result, Hagar started to despise her. Sarai started to treat Hagar so harshly that she ran away. The Angel found her at a well and told her to return home and submit to Sarai's authority (Genesis 16:9). The Angel told her that as a reward for her submission to her harsh leader, Hagar's descendants would be too numerous to count. What a reward! She had a choice to continue running, forfeiting the destiny God had for her, or return in obedience.

I have been in the place where I wanted to quit my job or leave the church due to mistreatment and I thank God for stopping me in my tracks. You do not want to leave the area of your assignment prematurely; keep serving your leaders until God releases you. The angel also told Hagar to name her son Ishmael which means "God hears," for He heard her pain. She declared, "You are the God who sees me" (Genesis 16:11,13). Be encouraged that God hears and sees everything you are going through.

Over the years, there have been times a leader has gotten angry at me and to be honest acted in the flesh. In those moments I knew I was called to be honorable and respectful despite how I was being treated. I could have blown up and gotten angry in response, but have you noticed that never helps the situation? In those moments, I quickly pray and ask God to give me the grace to be humble and honorable. Some of these leaders ended up apologizing to me later for their harsh words. I always think, "Wow, God really worked on their heart." It is incredible when God does that. That's why it is imperative you handle the situation correctly and put it in God's hands.

It's not about your feelings, it's about honoring God.

You are ultimately called to submit to God. If your leader or boss is asking you to stay late at work on a project or is not paying you what you think you should make, don't allow offense to grow in your heart. Instead, allow God to develop the character of Jesus in you and deal uprightly with leaders that are treating you unjustly. Ask the Lord to give you the wisdom to know if you are supposed to bring these issues forward, but don't move without the Spirit's guidance.

"Never pay back evil with more evil. Do things in such a way that everyone can see you are honorable. Do all that you can to live in peace with everyone... Don't let evil conquer you, but conquer evil by doing good." (Romans 12:17-18, 21)

When you act in the flesh, you are giving authority over to the enemy. When you act in the Spirit, you are giving authority back to God.

SYMPTOM #7
DESIRING YOUR
LEADER'S POSITION

Let's further examine the story of Korah. He incited a rebellion against Moses, but what was Korah really after? Moses' position. Korah was a Levite and had a prominent role in the community, but he desired more. He already had access to and the privilege of serving in the tabernacle, but that was not enough. He wanted more. Moses even asked him if all the ministry he was doing seemed insignificant to him. Moses then said,

> "Korah, He (God) has already given this special ministry to you and your fellow Levites. Are you now demanding the priesthood as well?" (Numbers 16:10)

Korah no longer viewed what he was doing as significant. He was now demanding the priesthood! This is scary. When people start desiring their leader's position, they start looking for ways to get it. Their loyalty and honor are now tainted. Rather than protecting their leader, they are looking for ways to get rid of them and take their place

ADONIJAH DESIRED KING SOLOMON'S POSITION

Toward the end of King David's life, his son Adonijah assumed the role of King. Solomon was supposed to succeed David as king, not Adonijah. Adonijah started boasting, "I will make myself king." That statement alone is disturbing. This type of attitude rears its head when people try to make things happen in the flesh rather than movement in the spirit by God. Adonijah went as far as buying a chariot, horses, and hired bodyguards. He put on this grand show and hosted a celebration for himself. They sacrificed cattle and fattened calves while drinking and shouting, "Long live King Adonijah!" The whole situation was out of control and his actions revealed the rebellious nature of his heart. He was determined to make himself King. His was dishonoring God and rebelling against the rightful authority.

ABSALOM DESIRED KING DAVID'S POSITION

Absalom was also one of David's sons who eagerly desired His father's position. Absalom would go to the city gate every morning to meet the people who were bringing their cases to the King for judgement. He would probe and ask them questions, acting like he really cared about them and they would end up telling him their case. He then told them,

> "I wish I were the judge. Then everyone could bring their cases to me for judgment, and I would give them justice!"... Absalom did this with everyone who came to the king for judgment, and so he stole the hearts of all the people of Israel." (2 Samuel 15:4, 6)

Absalom stole the hearts of David's followers to win their loyalty for himself and used his own agenda to try to seize the kingdom.

How It Ended for Korah, Absalom, and Adonijah: These three men sought to take their leader's positions, and each one faced harsh judgement as a result.

- The earth opened up and burned Korah and those with him.
- Adonijah was put to death by King Solomon.
- Absalom was killed with three arrows shot into his heart.

It is dangerous to desire your leader's position, and even more so to take action to obtain it. Rebellion always has a tragic ending.

"And no one can become a high priest simply because he wants such an honor. He must be called by God for this work, just as Aaron was. That is why Christ did not honor himself by assuming he could become High Priest. No, he was chosen by God." (Hebrews 5:4-5)

Jesus gave us the perfect example of how promotion works within the Kingdom. He did not honor Himself, He allowed God to choose Him and exalt Him. You never have to assume a position of authority; keep serving with a pure heart with pure motives, and let God fulfill all the plans He has for you.

EXAMINE YOUR MOTIVES

Not only is it dangerous to desire your leader's position, but dangerous when you start desiring titles. It's important to do regular heart checks: Are you serving with the motive of promotion, to get a leadership role or title? Do you only feel validated, valuable, or important when you have a title? Your value and self-worth should not come from a title but out of your relationship with God. The closer you draw near to God, the more you get to know Him and become like Him. Your value then is based on His love and not your works. I have watched people who served long hours and appeared to be faithful. Yet when they didn't get promoted or recognized like they thought they should have, they left the ministry or church. They fell into the trap of seeking a position and it became their motive for serving.

I have also seen people serve just to get close to the pastor. They feel they will be seen as a person of power and influence if they can be "in" with the pastor. These are the wrong motives for serving others because they are rooted in rebellion and greed. When your motive for serving comes from any place other than wanting to honor God, you have crossed into rebellion. I want to challenge you not to seek after titles or positions of authority. Those things will come in the right season. Our job is not to promote ourselves, that is God's job.

"Humble yourselves before the Lord, and he will lift you up in honor." (James 4:10)

SYMPTOM #8
CREATING DIVISION

When you look at all the prior symptoms we have discussed up until this point, they all reveal the most obvious symptom of dishonor and rebellion: creating division. All dishonor, all rebellion create division in the Body of Christ. The first incident of rebellion began in Heaven with Lucifer. He created division and deceived 1/3 of all of God's angels who were perfect beings. We are talking about at least a couple hundred thousand angels revolting against God. After God banished the fallen angels to hell and created the first man and women, Satan immediately sought to divide man from God, and he succeeded. This is why his ability to deceive is not to be taken lightly. We are dealing with an evil mastermind who has taken down kings, monarchs, presidents, and entire countries. He has destroyed families, and pastors of great churches. It is imperative that you and I understand our enemy and his tactics,

"Stay alert! Watch out for your great enemy, the devil. He prowls around like a roaring lion, looking for someone to devour."
(1 Peter 5:8)

Do we really understand what we're up against? Or do we have the mentality, "I have a fish symbol on the back of my car, I listen to Christian music so I'm good. Everything will work out." Many don't realize we are in a war, and we are up against an enemy capable of bombarding us with lies and deception. This is why we are called to,

"Put on all of God's armor so that you will be able to stand firm against all strategies of the devil." (Ephesians 6:11)

"All the strategies" implies there are a lot of different attacks we will go through. These attacks will be designed to target us in our weakest areas with the aim to take us out of the battle. Jesus told us that, "The thief's purpose is to steal and kill and destroy" (John 10:10).

It is imperative we know the enemy's attacks and strategies, and keep them at the forefront of our minds. His ultimate goal is to cause division between us and God, the church, our families, and our ministry leaders. Israel lost sight of this time and time again. Even though they suffered the consequences of dishonor many times, they kept falling back into rebellion. In Numbers 21, they became impatient and opted once again to complain and speak against God and Moses. Because of this divisive rebellion, God sent a plague of poisonous snakes through the camp and many died.

Their judgement was poison of the flesh because they were already poisoned in their spirits. May this open our eyes to the reality that a spirit of rebellion is a spirit that has been poisoned. This is why we are warned in the New Testament to, "Watch out that no poisonous root of bitterness grows up to trouble you, corrupting many" (Hebrews 12:15). When we get bitter or offended at our leaders and God, a poisonous root of bitterness grows inside our hearts and defiles us. The ultimate goal of the enemy is to stir a spirit of rebellion in your heart by poisoning it, for the purpose of creating division. He really doesn't care how this is accomplished. Every incident the Israelites went through caused division among God's people. Division has always been the Devil's end game.

DON'T GIVE IN TO DIVISION

Division breaks down the bond that holds the team together. Jesus said, "Every kingdom divided against itself is brought to desolation, and every city or house divided against itself will not stand" (Matthew 12:25 NKJV). We must fight for unity. A church or ministry team that is divided cannot and will not stand. Division comes in many ways and you must be on guard to it.

An associate pastor pulled me aside once and began talking to me about how our senior pastor was doing church leadership wrong and that church hierarchy was wrong. He proceeded to tell me how all levels of authority are equal. It didn't matter if you were the senior pastor or the church secretary. I immediately had a check in my spirit and told him I disagreed. This wasn't the first time this individual made dishonorable remarks to me about leadership.

I went home troubled that night from his conversation. My biggest concern was that if he was sharing his opinion with me, how many others was he sharing it with? A spirit of division spreads fast and will do damage quickly to team members. Nothing is worse than seeing godly people torn apart by a spirit of division. A spirit of division must always be confronted. It can not be swept under the carpet and forgotten.

As tempted as I was to ignore it and look the other way, this was a matter I knew I needed to share with our senior Pastor. I did not have direct authority over the associate pastor and thus needed our senior pastor to step in. They both had a meeting and our Pastor addressed the issue. Afterward, when the associate pastor came and met with me, he was broken and repented. He was actually grateful that I had brought it to the attention of our senior Pastor. He had been dealing with a prior offense and it was causing him to spread the divisive opinions. I was thankful I didn't ignore the situation; if I had, a divisive spirit would have continued to grow in his heart and could have spread to the rest of the Body.

The associate pastor fell prey to what anyone could easily fall into. It is easy for us to get slanted views or ideas of our leaders especially when we are offended. We must take care to deal with offences, laying them before the Lord daily. We must remember to act honorably even when mistreated so that our hearts aren't susceptible to Satan's divisive schemes. Paul warns us to,

> "Watch out for people who cause divisions… Stay away from them. Such people are not serving Christ our Lord; they are serving their own personal interest." (Romans 16:17-18)

People that cause division within a church are not serving the Lord. They have their own agenda for their own interests. If you see people like this, stay away from them. Don't spend time with them, these spirits seek control and they want to bring you in alignment with them to rebel. This is a dangerous trap that we must be aware of before we fall prey to it.

FIGHT FOR UNITY

It grieves my spirit when I see believers attack other believers on social media and tear down another ministry or other Christian leaders. Most of them do not realize that they are speaking from their flesh. Paul addressed the church and said, "So why do you condemn another believer? Why do you look down on another believer? Remember, we will all stand before the judgment seat of God" (Romans 14:10). We as the church can have disagreements and differences of opinion, but we must fight for unity. When we tear down other ministries, this gives fuel to darkness and does more damage in the world's eyes. We are a family. My sister and I can have disagreements, but I'm not going to publicly share those disagreements on social media or tear her down in front of other believers. As the church, we need to treat each other as family with honor, because ultimately the Lord is who we represent. Paul goes on to tell us, "So then, let us aim for harmony in the church and try to build each other up" (Romans 14:19).

When people choose unity, whether they are believers, nonbelievers, sports teams, or business teams, the results are the same: accomplishment. When people have one vision, they accomplish what they set out to do. The Tower of Babel is one of the best historical accounts to illustrate this point. A group of people set out to construct a building that would reach to the sky, a monument to their own greatness. They spoke one language and had one vision, read God's response,

"'Look!' he said. 'The people are united, and they all speak the same language. After this, nothing they set out to do will be impossible for them.'" (Genesis 11:6)

These were not believers of the one true God, but you can see that unity is unstoppable regardless of the group. How much more should the body of Christ be in one accord and have one vision? Just imagine what we could accomplish for the Kingdom! As a matter of fact, when believers come together, God commands a blessing on our work, so we can expect a blessing as the result.

"How wonderful and pleasant it is when brothers live together in harmony! For harmony is as precious as the anointing oil that was poured over Aaron's head, that ran down his beard and onto the border of his robe. Harmony (unity) is as refreshing as the dew from Mount Hermon that falls on the mountains of Zion. And there the LORD has pronounced his blessing, even life everlasting." (Psalm 133:1-3)

When there is discourse or division surrounding brothers and sisters, the Lord calls it an abomination (Proverbs 6:16,19). The Lord hates division because He knows the devastating effects it has on the church and its members.

Where there is no unity, there is no power.

He desires for you and I to experience the rewards that come from being in unity with the Body of Christ. These rewards are multiplied effectiveness, peace, anointing, blessing, and power through the Holy Spirit. We see the commanded blessing on the early church in Acts. All Christians at that time were of one heart and one soul. They honored one another above themselves and didn't fall into rebellion's snare. They shared all their material possessions. They considered nothing their own, they sold their houses and possessions to meet the needs of others in the church! The Bible says they operated in great grace and power, and there wasn't one person in the church lacking or in need because of this degree of generosity (see Acts 2:44-47, 4:32-37).

Can you even imagine what that was like? Can you imagine living in that kind of spirit of God's power? That is what real unity looks like. Some churches today feel cold and like a corporation, but this was not in any way shape or form how the early church was. They met daily; they ate together; they did life together. They were family. You may be at a church where you don't feel connected or feel like they are your family. If that's the case, let it start with you.

If you feel there is disunity in your ministry team, do everything in your power to bridge the gap. Even if the other individuals are not seeking reconciliation, make sure you are seeking reconciliation. If there is something you need to apologize for, humble yourself and do it. Even if you feel they have done you wrong, look for ways to show honor and appreciation toward them. Jesus commanded us to bless our enemies, yet most Christians really don't obey this command even with members of our local church! Think of writing a note of appreciation, getting them a gift card, or do something for them on their birthday.

"Love each other as brothers and sisters and honor others more than you do yourself." (Romans 12:10 CEV)

What would happen if the church did this today? What if we truly treated one another as brothers and sisters? I believe with all my heart what we saw in the book of Acts would take place and to a much greater extent. Take a look at the book of Acts and marvel at what God did through a unified Body:

- Acts 2:41 Three thousand were added to the church.
- Acts 2:47 Every single day people were getting saved.
- Acts 4:4   The Church grew to five thousand believers.
- Acts 5:14 Multitudes were added.
- Acts 5:28 Christians filled all Jerusalem with the gospel.
- Acts 6:1   There was rapid multiplication in converts.
- Acts 6:7   Disciples multiplied greatly.

Try to imagine that level of growth for a second. Entire cities were transformed at an accelerated rate. Huge numbers of people came to a saving faith in Christ every single day! They went from adding people to their numbers daily to multiplying them! Exponential growth is an unstoppable movement that takes place when believers are in unity and in alignment with the vision God has for the church. They honored one another more than themselves and began to walk in unity.

Unity is an unstoppable force.

SECTION 6: SUMMARY

SYMPTOM #5) Prideful Attitude: Pride makes you think you're stronger than you really are. When someone challenges their leaders, it is evident in their tone and attitude. They no longer speak with the utmost respect or love.

SYMPTOM #6) Blaming Your Leader: Oftentimes people will blame their leaders because they feel like their leaders are holding them back from their destiny. When this occurs, hearts become contaminated with dishonor and leaders begin to be viewed as the enemy. This path of rebellion is exactly what the devil wants to see, this path leads straight to dishonor.

SYMPTOM #7) Desiring Your Leader's Position: You never have to assume a position of authority; you keep serving with a pure heart with pure motives, and let God fulfill all the plans He has for you.

SYMPTOM #8) Creating Division: Of all the strategies the enemy uses, his main agenda is to create division on a team. This can come in many variations, but the end result is the same. Division breaks down the bond that holds the team together. Jesus said, "Every kingdom divided against itself is brought to desolation, and every city or house divided against itself will not stand" (Matthew 12:25 NKJV).

FIGHT FOR UNITY: God desires for you and I to experience the rewards that come from being in unity with the Body of Christ. These rewards are peace, anointing, blessing, and power through the Holy Spirit. Unity is where the Lord commands His blessing (Psalm 133:1-3).

SECTION 6: ACTION STEPS

1. Go to your ministry leader and ask them if they ever see you act in pride? Oftentimes this is a blind spot in people's lives. Take note of what they say and grow from it.

2. Ask them to keep you accountable in this area, that if they see you act out in pride or display an attitude of pride to bring it to your attention.

3. Have you felt mistreated by your leader? If so, go to God in prayer today and forgive them. Don't carry the offense and hurt any longer. Completely release it to God. Once you do, the Holy Spirit will bring healing to your heart.

4. Is there disunity on your ministry team? Pinpoint the reason(s). Prayerfully plan out your role in bringing unity to the team.

FULFILLING YOUR GOD-GIVEN DREAM

SECTION 7

⌐ WHAT ABOUT YOUR DREAMS AND CALLING? ⌐

Now that you've studied the 12 Kingdom Keys that cultivate a life of honor and learned to recognize that dishonor leads to the 8 Symptoms of Rebellion, I am confident your attitude towards authority is being greatly transformed. I pray that you are more excited than ever to serve your ministry leaders and God Himself. However, I know you may be wondering, "I have my own dreams and promises from God, what about those?" The dreams God gave you are to be treasured, it is essential you hold on to your dreams. Often the dreams God gives to us don't detail the process. Look at Joseph: he was given two vague dreams that he didn't fully understand. He had no idea what the process would entail in order for those dreams to come to fruition, or that it would take 12 years for them to come true! Oftentimes, when God gives us dreams that show us glimpses of our future calling, we want to run and make it happen immediately. We often don't realize that we still need to be refined, molded, and trained for the ministry.

God activates your gifting and calling when you serve the local church. Serving is the process by which we find the path to fulfill our God-given dreams. Serving breaks up the hardened soil of pride and plants seeds of humility which goes hand in hand with honor. As you continue to serve and be humbled, those seeds will grow. Look what Paul said about Timothy,

"You know how Timothy has proved himself. Like a son with his father, he has served with me in preaching the Good News." (Philippians 2:22)

Paul said Timothy served him like a son serves his father. Timothy's years of serving developed his character to be ready to become a senior pastor of Ephesus. Many today are not operating in their gifting and God given assignments because they have not served in God's house. While you serve your pastors and help fulfill the vision God has given them, God is refining your character. God is more concerned about your character being developed than your dreams being fulfilled.

"Until the time came to fulfill his dreams, the Lord tested Joseph's character." (Psalm 105:19)

The process that God doesn't reveal right away is the refining and molding that occurs as we walk through the storms and trials of life. The process where God turns up the heat and exposes areas in our lives that need to be burned out. God burns out our carnal nature with its fleshly desires and creates a pure heart. The process is necessary to be a qualified vessel ready to carry the anointing and authority for your calling and can take years. You cannot be trusted until you have been tested.

The Most Difficult Test:
Are you serving God or your dream?

I can assure you at some point you will go through this test. Look what God did with Abraham, He told him to take his son and kill him. Now this made absolutely no natural sense because Isaac was the promised child, he was the dream. God tested Abraham to see what the first priority in his life was. The promise or God? Abraham passed the test, and God said, "Now I know that you truly fear God" (Genesis 22:12).

Joseph was given a dream and then immediately became a slave and prisoner. I don't care how you look at it, you and I would have never thought that was the career path to the palace. These Biblical examples instruct us to follow God and not our dreams. There was a man that served for a brief time on our team who had a call on his life to be a pastor. He had made mistakes in his past that cost him his marriage. As tragic as that was, he still had the call of God on his life, because giftings and callings are irrevocable (Romans 11:29). He acknowledged his mistakes and joined our hospitality team. He said he wanted to get back to serving God. This ministry involved picking up guest speakers and assisting them while they were at the church. After serving a guest speaker coffee he said, "Is this all I'm going to be doing, serving people coffee? I'm called to be a pastor."

He threw in the towel and quit the hospitality team that day. He didn't want to be the servant. He wanted to be the pastor. This grieved my spirit deeply. His whole way of thinking was backwards. If he only realized pastors and leaders are all servants, just as Jesus was. All leaders start out serving, and are promoted by God because of their humble servanthood, and they continue to serve till the end.

Serving is the vehicle and Honor is the fuel that will drive you to your destiny.

Some think if they just go to Bible school and get a ministry degree, the doors will open for them. However, head knowledge without heart transformation is vain and only leads to pride. I'm all for Bible and ministry schooling; studying and showing yourself approved is important. The reality is, having a degree in theology will not propel you into your calling, unless you earn a Master's degree in serving! This degree is not an accolade you hang on your wall, rather it's engraved on your heart. There is no ceremony for this, no applause or recognition except from Jesus Himself!

DON'T RUSH YOUR CALLING

I believe one of the biggest challenges and temptations we battle is rushing our calling. Patience is not in our sin nature. We want everything right now. There are things God wants us to have, but there is a perfect timing for everything. David was prophesied and anointed king somewhere between the age of 10-15 years old. David didn't march into the King's palace and demand Saul hand over his crown to a teenager. He could have done this and even declared, "God has anointed me!" But he didn't. David did not become King of Judah until he was 30 years old and did not become King over all Israel until he was 37. This means David waited 22-27 years for his calling to come to pass. Rather than demanding to be King as a child who would have had no idea how to be king, he served King Saul as his musician, armor bearer and then as high-ranking commander before being promoted to King.

> "So David went to Saul and began serving him. Saul loved
> David very much, and David became his armor bearer."
> (1 Samuel 16:21)

David had a chance to rush his calling at the end of Saul's reign, when things started to go badly with their relationship. King Saul had become full of pride and jealousy over David's victories, to the point of wanting to kill him. David had to flee to the wilderness. Saul received David's location and pursued him with 3,000 soldiers.

> "Now's your opportunity!" David's men whispered to him. "Today the Lord is telling you, 'I will certainly put your enemy into your power, to do with as you wish.'" So David crept forward and cut off a piece of the hem of Saul's robe. But then David's conscience began bothering him because he had cut Saul's robe. He said to his men, "The Lord forbid that I should do this to my lord

the king. I shouldn't attack the Lord's anointed one, for the Lord himself has chosen him." So David restrained his men and did not let them kill Saul." (1 Samuel 24:4-7)

Those around David told him, "Now is your opportunity!" This could not have been further from the truth. Thank God David was sensitive to his conscience and restrained himself from rushing his calling. When Saul came out of the cave, David yelled out to him and knelt. He began pouring out his heart: "I have not sinned against you, there is neither evil nor rebellion in my hand, I will never harm you, and you are the Lord's anointed one." One of the most amazing things happened, Saul started weeping, and with tears running down his face he said to David, "Now I know indeed that you shall surely be king, and that the kingdom of Israel shall be established in your hand" (v20). David's honor influenced Saul's heart and paved the way directly to the fulfillment of God's call on David's life.

God will reveal your calling to your leaders through your honor.

WRONG TIMING

I have a good friend who felt called to be a youth pastor, similar to the young man I spoke of a few chapters ago. He was serving in the youth ministry at our church, but always felt called to be a youth pastor. One afternoon, he called me excitedly and wanted to talk. He shared the news with me that a church wanted him to become their youth pastor. I was immediately flooded with the thought that he was not ready. I asked him, "Have you spoken to our youth pastor about this?" He said, "Yes, but he was not supportive of the move." This didn't surprise me.

This young man told me how this was God opening the door for him, and this was his dream coming true. He said his youth pastor was wrong and couldn't see what God was doing in his life. As a mentor in his life I had to tell him he should turn down the position and keep serving in his current youth ministry. I realized he didn't want to hear from me either. I have learned, that when someone is infected with a spirit of dishonor and rebellion; they will try to get a "yes" from someone else after their leader has told them "no".

> *If you have to dishonor your leader to get your opportunity, it is not your opportunity! If you have to rebel to get your promotion, it is not your promotion. The timing is off.*

This young man chose a path of dishonor towards his leaders and left our church to pursue this dream from God, or so he thought. Just like the first young man I spoke of, things quickly went downhill for him. He got involved with a girl, got married, then divorced in less than a year. He eventually came back to our church broken by the experience. He never did regain the servanthood he had prior to leaving. He now attends the church from time to time, but I look back on that situation and wish he had never gone. Some people get detoured from their calling by attempting to fulfill it at the wrong time.

GOD'S TIMING

God's timing is drastically different than ours. This is why Peter tells us, "You must not forget this one thing, dear friends: A day is like a thousand years to the Lord, and a thousand years is like a day" (2 Peter 3:8). This means one hour to God is forty-one years of our time. Let's break it down a little more: Six months is like one minute to God. I remember dreams God gave me when I was a teenager. I was convinced those dreams would be fulfilled in the next two or three years. I was way off,

some of them are just starting to break ground 15-20 years later.
Be encouraged that:

- Elisha waited for 7 years for a double portion of the anointing
- Joseph waited 12 years to fulfill his dreams
- David waited 22+ years for the fulfilment of his calling
- Abraham waited 25 years for his promise to come to pass

God gives us the dream, then calls us to honor our leaders through service as He refines our character in preparation to fulfill that dream. God then moves in the heart of our leaders to anoint and send us in peace, power, and authority. Peter gives us clear direction on how to prepare ourselves as we wait for God to fulfill our dreams.

"In the same way, you who are younger must accept the authority of the elders. And all of you, dress yourselves in humility as you relate to one another, for "God opposes the proud but gives grace to the humble." So humble yourselves under the mighty power of God, and at the right time he will lift you up in honor."
(1 Peter 5:5-6)

In the right time God will raise you up, in the meantime, humble yourself and build your leaders vision. If you build your leader's vision, God will build yours, and He will bring what's in your heart to pass in ways you can't even fathom. In Ephesians, right after Paul gives instructions on how to serve our leaders, he then encourages us with "knowing that whatever good anyone does, he will receive the same from the Lord" (Ephesians 6:8 NKJV).

What you make happen for others,
God will make happen for you!

WHAT IF GOD SPEAKS TO ME?

I have no doubt God speaks to you and shares insights with you as His child. He has grand plans in store for you and loves to share His wisdom. That being said, let me give you a bit of wisdom that will serve as a safety net for you. When you feel God is speaking to you about your calling or assignment, go talk it over with your pastor. Your pastor would love to hear what God is saying to you. Listen to their counsel and advice on the matter. Remember you are called to obey your leader (Hebrews 13:17). Wait until they send you with a blessing. If God spoke to you, He will confirm it through the leaders He has appointed in your life.

There is a night and day difference between those who leave a church to pursue their calling in honor rather than dishonor. Would you prefer to go in your ability or be sent with God's authority? Consider Moses, God spoke to him through the burning bush. He had an undeniably powerful encounter with God about going to Egypt and fulfilling his calling by delivering the Hebrews. The first thing Moses did after this encounter was go to Jethro who was the Priest of Midian and asked for his permission to return to Egypt. He honored Jethro and Jethro said, "Go in peace" (Exodus 4:18 NLT). There is a powerful principle here: go in peace.

When you are sent by your leadership, the timing is right, you proceed with blessing, authority, honor and peace. You advance with the tools you need, and have been prepared for the battle.

GOD WILL RAISE YOU UP!

A few years ago, I caught a glimpse of the Olympics on television. I realized that every one of those athletes passionately desired to be there, planned to be there, and even more specifically prepared to be there. They had given their entire lives to the goal of becoming an Olympian. They made tremendous sacrifices and designed strict regimen for their daily lives to ensure they hit their benchmarks. They disciplined their bodies in every way possible: dieting, working out, and practicing. They do all this for a medal that will eventually become dusty, sitting on display somewhere in their home only to be a distant memory.

"All athletes are disciplined in their training. They do it to win a prize that will fade away, but we do it for an eternal prize. So I run with purpose in every step. I am not just shadowboxing. I discipline my body like an athlete, training it to do what it should. Otherwise, I fear that after preaching to others I myself might be disqualified." (1 Corinthians 9:25-27)

How much more devout, intentional and passionate should we be as believers when it comes to fulfilling our calling? As Christians, we should be laser focused on bringing the gift of Jesus to the masses because we are doing it for an eternal prize. We should be disciplining ourselves like champion athletes, running with purpose in every step. Honor is the path we must run on.

"Therefore I, a prisoner for serving the Lord, beg you to lead a life worthy of your calling, for you have been called by God." (Ephesians 4:1)

All athletes must follow the rules of their competition regardless of how gifted they are. A big part of those rules includes honoring the coaches, the authorities in any given sport. Some of the greatest athletes never make it to the pro level because they won't follow the rules. When I was in high school, I was at a park playing basketball with one of the most talented players I had personally ever played with. He had the potential to get a college scholarship and possibly a shot at the pros. I asked him, "Why aren't you on the basketball team at school?" He responded that he didn't like the coaches at school and didn't care for organized basketball. I remember being shocked by his response. His opportunity to have huge success was lost, all because he was unwilling to conform to the rules.

"Athletes cannot win the prize unless they follow the rules." (2 Timothy 2:5)

Our gifting does not take precedence over following the rules. As believers, we have rules we must follow to win our prize. Our organization, the Kingdom of God, is far superior to any athletic organization. We have coaches that God has placed in our lives to train us and build us up. One of the most important rules of our organization is the mandate to honor our leaders.

If we run without honor,
we will be disqualified from the race.

As you continue your journey remember that Jesus appointed the apostle, prophet, pastor, teacher and evangelist and their job is to equip people for ministry (Ephesians 4:11). God will use your ministry leaders to impart spiritual gifts to you and those leaders will release you to function in your calling when you are proven faithful (see Romans 1:11, 2 Timothty 1:6, 2:2).

GOD HOLDS YOUR LEADERS HEART

"The king's heart is a stream of water in the hand of the LORD; he turns it wherever he will." (Proverbs 21:1 ESV)

I want you to hold on to this verse in the upcoming months and seasons of you serving. This verse has brought tremendous relief to me whenever I found myself struggling with Kingdom Honor in obeying and serving my leaders. It's normal for us to feel the struggle of "does my pastor see the calling on my life? Does he care? Will he ever help me fulfill my call? What if He doesn't listen to God in regard to my call?" Verses like Proverbs 21:1 should remind you that God is in control of your future. He is the one that will promote you when the time is right. He has not forgotten the dreams He gave you. Look at how God can move through unrighteous leader's hearts:

- He hardened Pharaoh's heart to display His power through Moses.
- He moved in Pharaoh's heart to promote Joseph.
- He used King Nebuchadnezzar to promote Daniel, Shadrach, Meshach, and Abednego.
- He promoted Daniel through King Darius.
- He promoted Mordecai through King Xerxes.
- He promoted David through King Saul.

If God did this through ungodly leaders, He surely does this through godly leaders as well:

- He used Moses to promote Joshua.
- He used Samuel to appoint Saul.
- He used Elijah to raise up Elisha.
- He used Paul to train and mentor Timothy.

These men remained servants and waited until God moved in the hearts of their leaders to promote them. God's perfect timing. Could you imagine if these men tried in their own timing to make their callings come to pass? We quite possibly would have never heard about them or read a completely different outcome of their lives. You can trust God to move in the heart of your leader to promote you and fulfill your dreams when the time is right. Until then, remember to make their dreams your own.

God used all of these leaders to accomplish His will and plans on the earth, and He will continue to use leaders however He sees fit. You can rest on the promise that no one can ruin your calling or destiny. No corrupt leader, your enemies, nor Satan himself can stop you as long as you remain a vessel of honor. Honor God by honoring His delegated authority in your life. Serve your leaders exceptionally well. Humble your heart and do the work set before you in this season. Guard your heart and stay in His Holy Word. Watch yourself for signs of rebellion and root them out if they emerge.

As I've mentioned before, I spent seven years serving as my pastor's assistant. These years molded my character, transformed my heart, and equipped me for ministry. As I neared the completion of this book, God moved in the heart of my pastor to promote me to associate pastor. I am so grateful for my years of serving him and for the opportunity to continue in ministry as a servant leader. I have shared everything I have learned with you in this book. I pray you can use the Kingdom Keys to encourage you and to equip you for the journey. I pray you will use your knowledge of rebellion's symptoms to guard your heart, your ministry, and your leaders. It is the greatest desire of my heart that you live out a lifestyle dedicated to honor, serving your local church, and the leaders God has placed in your life.

Never forget this verse and principle:

"Humble yourselves under the mighty power of God, and at the right time he will lift you up in honor." (1 Peter 5:6)

God will raise you up through honor!

SECTION 7: SUMMARY

1. The dreams God gave you are to be treasured and valued, and it is essential you hold on to your dreams. Often the dreams God gives to us don't include the process. Look at Joseph. Until the time came to fulfill his dreams, the Lord tested Joseph's character. (Psalm 105:19)

2. The process is where God turns up the heat and exposes areas in our lives that need to be burned out. God burns out our carnal nature with its fleshly desires and creates a pure heart. This process is necessary to be a qualified vessel to carry the anointing and authority for your calling and can take years.

3. If you have to dishonor your leader to get your opportunity, it is not your opportunity! If you have to be dishonorable to get your promotion, it is not your promotion. The timing is off.

4. No one can stop you from fulfilling God's calling on your life, but you. If you allow God to refine and take you through the process of becoming a vessel of honor, God will raise you up!

SECTION 7: ACTION STEPS

1. Write down the dreams God has given you and don't ever lose sight of them.

2. Meet with your leader and share the dreams you have. It's important your leader knows what God has spoken to you. Let them know you're not going to pursue those or try to make them happen in your own timing, but wait for their blessing when the time is right.

3. Memorize this scripture:

"Humble yourselves under the mighty power of God, and at the right time he will lift you up in honor." (1 Peter 5:6)

NOTES

TIME TO BRING HONOR BACK

1. The meaning of the word honor:

   https://www.blueletterbible.org/lang/lexicon/lexicon.cfm?t=kjv&strongs=g5092

   https://www.blueletterbible.org/lang/lexicon/lexicon.cfm?strongs=G5091&t=KJV

2. Here are some startling statistics on ministry leaders:

   http://www.churchleadership.org/apps/articles/default.asp?blogid=4545&view=post&articleid=Statistics-on-Pastors-2016-Update&link=1&fldKeywords=&fldAuthor=&fldTopic=0

3. The Greek word for Kingdom is basileia:

   https://www.blueletterbible.org/lang/lexicon/lexicon.cfm?Strongs=G932&t=KJV

4. Other definitions:

   https://www.merriam-webster.com/dictionary/honor

   https://www.dictionary.com/browse/honor

THE IMPACT OF DISHONOR

1. The Greek definition for the word hindered is "to cut off"

   https://www.blueletterbible.org/lang/lexicon/lexicon.cfm?Strongs=G1581&t=KJV

THE IMPORTANCE OF CHURCH AUTHORITY

1. "Each ruler of the great empires of the world was, in ways he knew

not, working out the purposes of God." Ellicott's Commentary
https://www.studylight.org/commentaries/ebc/jeremiah-25.html

2. "So the wicked and Satan himself are God's servants, because he makes them serve him by constraint and turns that which they do out of malice to his honor and glory." Geneva Study Bible

    https://www.biblestudytools.com/commentaries/geneva-study-bible/jeremiah/jeremiah-25.html

KEY #1: BECOME A VESSEL OF HONOR

1. The word holy1 used in this verse means to be sanctified: to separate from profane things and dedicate to God

    https://www.blueletterbible.org/lang/lexicon/lexicon.cfm?Strongs=G37&t=KJV

2. The Greek word for pursuit is diōkō. It is a passionate seeking; it is aggressive, intentional and eager.

    https://www.blueletterbible.org/lang/lexicon/lexicon.cfm?Strongs=G1377&t=KJV

3. The Hebrew word for heart is Leb: seat of appetites, seat of emotions and seat of passion https://www.blueletterbible.org/lang/lexicon/lexicon.cfm?Strongs=H3820&t=KJV

4. I read recently that the average gamer is in his 30's

    https://www.myhighplains.com/news/tech-news/the-average-age-of-a-video-gamer/

5. Recent porn stats show that 79% of men look at porn monthly and 34% of women between the ages of 18-30.

    https://www.churchmilitant.com/news/article/new-survey-of-porn-use-shows-startling-stats-for-men-and-women

https://www.provenmen.org/pornography-survey-statistics-2014/
https://fightthenewdrug.org/survey-finds-one-in-three-women-watch-porn-at-least-once-a-week/

KINGDOM KEY #2: DEVELOP A SERVANTS HEART

1. To get a brief understanding of what it means to be great, the Greek word Jesus used was megas which means:

   https://www.blueletterbible.org/lang/lexicon/lexicon.cfm Strongs=G3173&t=KJV

KINGDOM KEY #4: RESPECT YOUR LEADER

1. The meaning of the word honor:

   https://www.blueletterbible.org/lang/lexicon/lexicon.cfm?t=k jv&strongs=g5092

   https://www.blueletterbible.org/lang/lexicon/lexicon. cfm?strongs=G5091&t=KJV

KINGDOM KEY #6: SERVE YOUR LEADER LIKE YOU WOULD SERVE JESUS

1. This word enthusiasm also means zeal, passion, and excitement. https://www.merriam-webster.com/dictionary/enthusiasm

KINGDOM KEY #7: CULTIVATE AND EXCELLENT SPIRIT

1. The particular word used in this verse for abilities was the Greek word dýnamis meaning: Strength, ability, and power.

   https://www.blueletterbible.org/lang/lexicon/lexicon.cfm Strongs=G1411&t=KJV

KINGDOM KEY #9: GIVE DOUBLE HONOR

1. A poll states 57% of pastors can't pay their bills.

   http://www.churchleadership.org/apps/articles/default.as p?blogid=4545&view=post&articleid=Statistics-on-Pastors -2016-Update&link=1&fldKeywords=&fldAuthor=&fldTopic=0

2. On top of this, their financial pressures are weighing them down. Recent stats say: 63% of pastor's wives feel finances are a prime source of stress for their family.

   http://www.churchleadership.org/apps/articles/default.as
   p?blogid=4545&view=post&articleid=Statistics-on-Pastors
   -2016-Update&link=1&fldKeywords=&fldAuthor=&fld
   Topic=0

3. Financial stress is a leading cause of divorce
   https://www.daveramsey.com/pr/money-ruining-marriages-in-america

KINGDOM KEY #10: GUARD YOUR LEADERS

1. This year in 2020 Barna stats predict 20% of churches will close down within in the next 18 months.

   https://www.christianpost.com/news/1-in-5-churches-face-closure-within-18-months-due-to-covid-19-shutdowns-barna-president.html

2. Here are some additional statistics for ministry leaders:

   http://www.churchleadership.org/apps/articles/default.as
   p?blogid=4545&view=post&articleid=Statistics-on-Pastors
   -2016-Update&link=1&fldKeywords=&fldAuthor=&fldTopic=0

3. The Hebrew word used in this verse for the word "guards" is shamar:

   https://www.blueletterbible.org/lang/lexicon/lexicon.
   cfm?Strongs=H8104&t=KJV

4. Today 26% of ministry leaders are overly fatigued:
   http://www.churchleadership.org/apps/articles/default.as
   p?blogid=4545&view=post&articleid=Statistics-on-Pastors
   -2016-Update&link=1&fldKeywords=&fldAuthor=&fldTopic=0

5. While 91% have experienced some form of burnout during their ministry.

   https://www.soulshepherding.org/pastors-under-stress/

6. Most ministry leaders are pushing themselves to work 55-75 hours a week.

   https://shepherdswatchmen.com/browse-all-posts/statistics-concerning-pastoral-needs/

7. A recent poll stated 34% of ministry leaders battle discouragement and 43% are overstressed.

   http://www.churchleadership.org/apps/articles/default.as
   p?blogid=4545&view=post&articleid=Statistics-on-Pastors
   -2016-Update&link=1&fldKeywords=&fldAuthor=&fldTopic=0

KINGDOM KEY #11: PRAY FOR YOUR LEADERS DAILY

1. Monday evening November 25, 2019 my pastor had a cardiac arrest in our church parking lot, 94% of people do not survive these.

   http://www8.nationalacademies.org/onpinews/newsitem.aspx?Recor
   dID=21723

KINGDOM KEY #12: HONOR THE WORD

1. Several polls reveal that most Christians are not spending daily time in The Word.

   https://www.premierchristianity.com/Blog/Only-9-of-Christian-Mil
   lennials-read-the-Bible-daily.-And-we-ve-only-got-ourselves-to-
   blame

   https://factsandtrends.net/2019/07/02/how-many-protestant-church
   goers-actually-read-the-bible-regularly/

   https://www.christianitytoday.com/news/2012/september/
   80-of-churchgoers-dont-read-bible-daily-lifeway-survey.html

2. A recent article stated that only 9% of Christian millennials read the Bible daily.

   https://www.premierchristianity.com/Blog/Only-9-of-Christian-Millennials-read-the-Bible-daily.-And-we-ve-only-got-ourselves-to-blame

3. Strong's definition for desire: intensely crave possession.

   https://www.blueletterbible.org/lang/lexicon/lexicon.cfm?Strongs=G1971&t=KJV

THE SPIRITUAL SICKNESS

1. (re·bel·lion) resistance to or defiance of any authority
   Synonyms: uprising, revolt, defiance, disobedience, insubordination.

   https://www.dictionary.com/browse/rebellion?s=t

2. When you look at the pioneers that traveled across the United States a few hundred years ago, they covered between 15-20 miles a day on average.

   https://www.history.com/news/9-things-you-may-not-know-about-the-oregon-trail

MINISTRY RESOURCES

Great for individual use or group studies

PAPERBACK & HARDCOPY

E-BOOK

AUDIO BOOK

VIDEO & AUDIO COURSE

KINGDOMHONOR.COM

STAY CONNECTED
ON SOCIAL MEDIA

@GARYJMONTOYA

@GARY.JOSEPH.MONTOYA

Printed in Great Britain
by Amazon

66897950R00139